T0220323

The Absolute Beginner's Guide to HTML and CSS

A Step-by-Step Guide with Examples and Lab Exercises

Kevin Wilson

Apress®

The Absolute Beginner's Guide to HTML and CSS: A Step-by-Step Guide with Examples and Lab Exercises

Kevin Wilson
WIDNES, UK

ISBN-13 (pbk): 978-1-4842-9249-5   ISBN-13 (electronic): 978-1-4842-9250-1
https://doi.org/10.1007/978-1-4842-9250-1

Managing Director, Apress Media LLC: Welmoed Spahr
Acquisitions Editor: James Robinson-Prior
Development Editor: James Markham
Coordinating Editor: Gryffin Winkler

Cover designed by eStudioCalamar

Cover image designed by vectorjuice on Freepik

Distributed to the book trade worldwide by Springer Science+Business Media New York, 1 New York Plaza, Suite 4600, New York, NY 10004-1562, USA. Phone 1-800-SPRINGER, fax (201) 348-4505, e-mail orders-ny@springer-sbm.com, or visit www.springeronline.com. Apress Media, LLC is a California LLC and the sole member (owner) is Springer Science + Business Media Finance Inc (SSBM Finance Inc). SSBM Finance Inc is a **Delaware** corporation.

For information on translations, please e-mail booktranslations@springernature.com; for reprint, paperback, or audio rights, please e-mail bookpermissions@springernature.com.

Apress titles may be purchased in bulk for academic, corporate, or promotional use. eBook versions and licenses are also available for most titles. For more information, reference our Print and eBook Bulk Sales web page at http://www.apress.com/bulk-sales.

Any source code or other supplementary material referenced by the author in this book is available to readers on GitHub via https://github.com/Apress.

Printed on acid-free paper

Table of Contents

About the Author

With over 20 years of experience in the computer industry, **Kevin Wilson** has made a career out of technology and is showing others how to use it. After earning a master's degree in computer science, software engineering, and multimedia systems, Kevin has held various positions in the IT industry including graphic and web design, digital film and photography, programming and software engineering, developing and managing corporate networks, building computer systems, and IT support. He currently teaches computer science at college and works as an IT trainer in England while researching for his Ph.D.

About the Technical Reviewer

Jonathon Simpson is a product owner and engineer living in the UK. He graduated from UCL in 2015. With many years of experience, he has developed and run many successful projects both independently and in large companies. He produces a popular software engineering blog called fjolt.com and posts regular newsletters about the latest developments and trends in JavaScript and web development.

Introduction

The aim of this book is to provide a first course in the use of HTML and CSS.

It provides a foundation for those who wish to develop their own websites, and because the book is intended to be a primer, it allows the beginner to become comfortable with basic HTML and CSS coding.

As it is a first course, no previous experience of computer programming is assumed.

Throughout the book, we'll explore HTML and CSS with worked examples and lab exercises for you to complete yourself. We'll also introduce JavaScript and how it can be used to add interactivity to a website, as well as using content management systems such as WordPress. For this purpose, we've included all the source code for this book in the following repository: `https://github.com/Apress/The-Absolute-Beginner-s-Guide-to-HTML-and-CSS`

CHAPTER 1

Getting Started

Originally developed in the early 1990s by Tim Berners-Lee, HTML stands for HyperText Markup Language and is a language used to lay out and format documents for the World Wide Web that are designed to be displayed in a web browser. In other words, the HTML code describes the structure of a web page. HTML can be used with other technologies such as Cascading Style Sheets (CSS) to style and format the document and scripting languages such as JavaScript to provide functionality and interactive elements.

Basic knowledge of HTML is essential for students and anyone working in web development. This will help you

- Understand the World Wide Web.

- Create and customize your own websites: You can create a website or customize an existing web template if you know HTML.

- Become a web developer: If you want to start a career as a professional web developer, HTML and CSS are essential skills.

Linking Pages Together

Web pages are all linked together using clickable text or images, called hyperlinks. This is known as hypertext and enables you to create multiple pages on a website that allow the user to browse through the pages by clicking these hyperlinks.

© Kevin Wilson 2023
K. Wilson, *The Absolute Beginner's Guide to HTML and CSS*,
https://doi.org/10.1007/978-1-4842-9250-1_1

Hyperlinks can also link to pages and resources hosted on other websites.

The links can be embedded into the body of a paragraph as an underlined word or as an image or icon. This is called hypertext.

As you can see in Figure 1-1, on the left, the hyperlinks appear in light blue text. When you click the link, the browser will take you to the linked page.

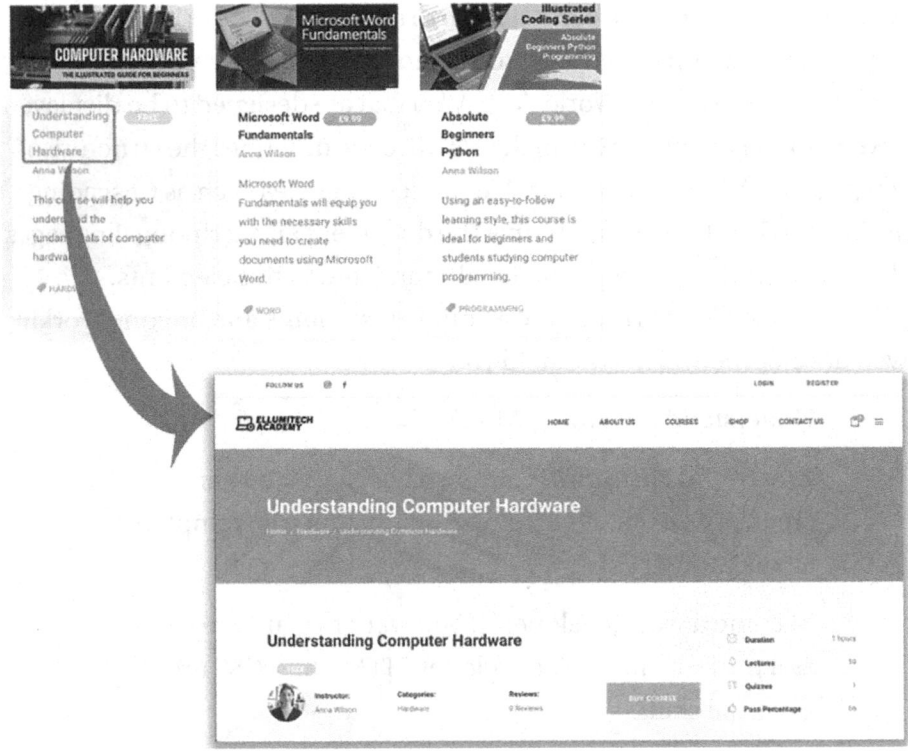

Figure 1-1. *Hypertext Document*

Where Are Web Pages Stored?

A website and its pages are stored or hosted on a web server. Web servers are computers usually running Windows Server or, more commonly, some flavor of the Linux operating system such as CentOS. Running on these machines is a piece of software called a web server. This is usually Apache, IIS, or NGINX (pronounced "Engine X").

What Is a URL?

Each website on the World Wide Web has an address called a URL (Figure 1-2) or Uniform Resource Locator.

Figure 1-2. Anatomy of a URL

The URL itself can be broken down into its basic elements. Let's take a closer look at an example:

```
https://www.ellumitechacademy.com
```

The "www.ellumitechacademy.com" part is called the hostname.

Let's break the URL down into its different parts.

https:// stands for hypertext transfer protocol secured and is the protocol the web browser is using to connect to the server. This is known as the scheme.

You might find other schemes such as ftp:// if you are connecting to an FTP site.

www is the name of the server hosting the service or subdomain, in this case www for the World Wide Web, and usually points to your public_html or htdocs directory on the web server.

This can also be another service such as an email server:

`mail.`ellumitechacademy.com

or perhaps a subdomain for the website's online store:

`shop.`ellumitechacademy.com

ellumitechacademy is the domain name or organization's name and is unique to that organization. This is known as a second-level domain.

.com is the type of site. It can be .co.*x* for country-specific companies (e.g., .co.uk), .org for nonprofit organizations, or .gov for government organizations. These are known as top-level domain names and are designed to identify the types of companies represented on the Web.

After the domain name, you might find a forward slash, then another name. This is known as a subdirectory or path. For example, to access the courses directory on the web server, we'd use

`www.ellumitechacademy.com/courses`

or for an html directory inside courses, we'd use

`www.ellumitechacademy.com/courses/html`

If we want to access a web page or a file for download, we add the path and file name of the file or document:

`www.ellumitechacademy.com/aboutus.html`

or a file in the downloads directory:

`www.ellumitechacademy.com/downloads/menu.pdf`

Of course, these files and directories would need to exist in the public_ html or htdocs directory on the web server (Figure 1-3). Here, we can see the courses and downloads directories on the server.

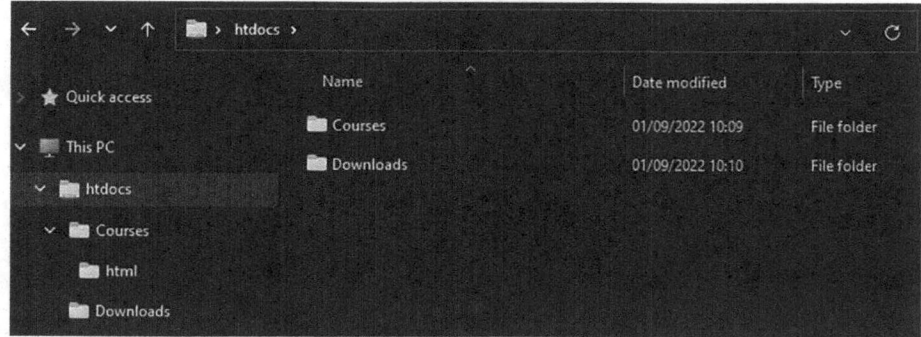

Figure 1-3. *Directory Structure on a Web Server*

Index Pages

Websites are built inside directories on a web server. The index file is the default page displayed if no other page is specified when a visitor enters the URL into their web browser. This index file could be index.html, index. php, or index.py depending on which language you're using to develop your site. For now, we'll use index.html.

In our example, we have a directory structure on our web server (Figure 1-4).

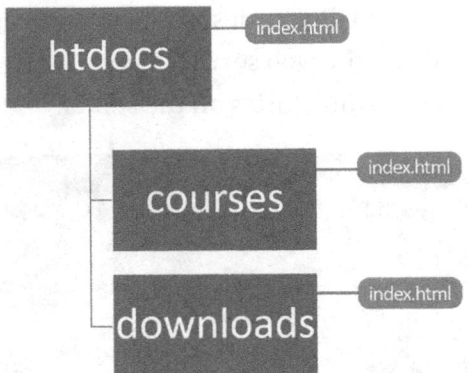

Figure 1-4. *Directory Structure*

Inside the directory, you'd have an index file that is displayed by default when the user navigates to the directory in their browser. If the user types in

`www.ellumitechacademy.com/courses`

the web server will look in the directory for the index.html file:

`www.ellumitechacademy.com/courses/index.html`

If the index.html file is missing, the web server will attempt to display a list of files, or you'll see an error message (Figure 1-5).

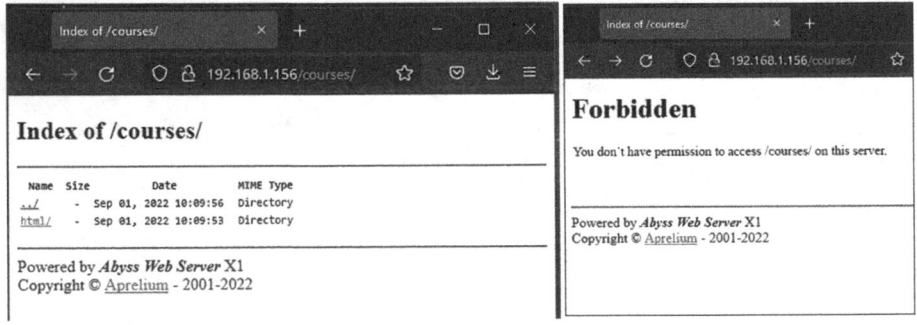

Figure 1-5. *Web Server Directory Listing*

HTML5

HTML5 brings device independence, meaning websites can be developed for all different types of platforms, from PCs to smartphones, without the need to endlessly install plugins on your browser or develop multiple versions of a website for mobile devices as we can see in Figure 1-6.

Figure 1-6. *Website on Different Devices*

HTML5 also introduces some new tags to handle page structure such as <section>, <head>, <nav>, <aside>, and <footer> and some tags to handle media such as <audio> or <video>.

We'll take a look at some of the new HTML5 features later in this guide.

What Is CSS?

Cascading Style Sheets (CSS) are used to define and customize the styles and layout for your web pages. This means you can create style sheets to alter the design, layout, and responsiveness to different screen sizes on various devices from computers to smartphones.

In CSS, selectors declare which part of the HTML markup a style applies. The selector could be an H1 heading style, a body tag, or a paragraph tag.

So what you'll see is a selector, say H1, and inside the curly braces, you'll see a declaration block where you declare your styles for that selector (Figure 1-7).

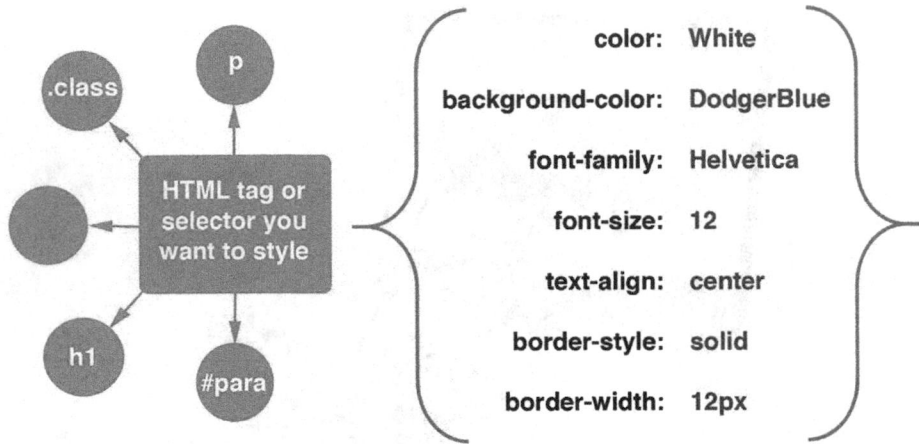

Figure 1-7. *Anatomy of a CSS Selector*

You can either add your CSS declarations to the <head> section of your HTML document between the <style>...</style> tags or add your CSS declarations to a separate style.css file and add a link in the <head> section of your HTML document using

```
<link rel="stylesheet" type="text/css" href="styles.css">
```

This is a better way since it allows you to change the styles in one place rather than in each HTML page you create.

We'll take a closer look at CSS later in Chapter 4 of this book.

Hosting

For hosting your website, you have three options:

- A dedicated hosting service, where a server located at your school or is provided for your use. This can be used for development and in some cases a live website depending on the service.

- Setting up a personalized web server on your own computer: This is only good for testing and development and is not intended to host a live website.

- Managed hosting service or web host, which is a service managed by a web hosting provider: This is what you would use to host a live website that is available publicly.

Installing Our Web Server

In this guide, we are going to use a personal web server. This will help you set up a development environment you can use on your computer to test your website without having it accessible on the Internet.

Abyss turns your computer in a full-featured web server. To download Abyss Web Server, open a web browser and navigate to

`aprelium.com/downloads`

On the left-hand side, click "Free Download" (Figure 1-8).

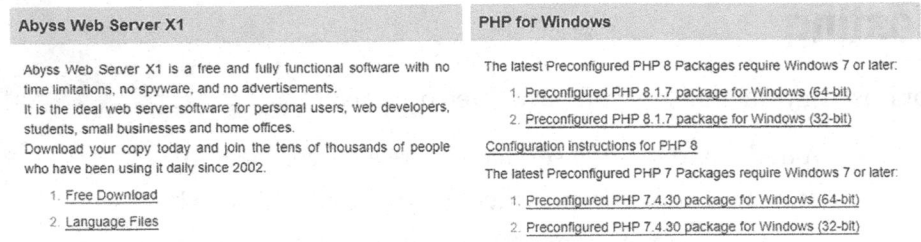

Figure 1-8. *Download Web Page*

Select the Windows version (or the Mac version if you're using a Mac) (Figure 1-9).

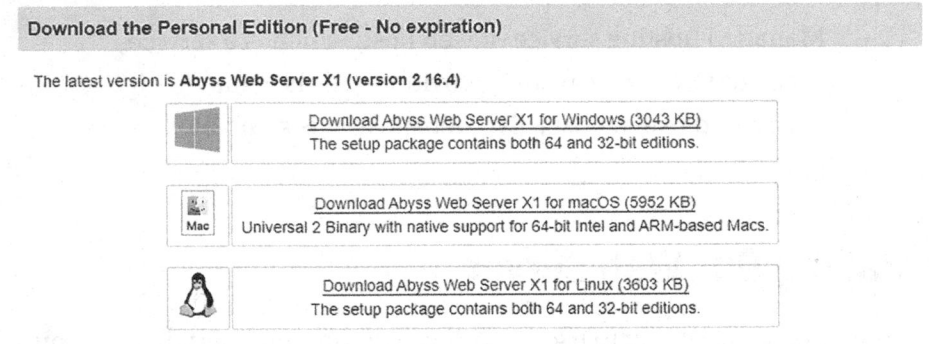

Figure 1-9. *Download Abyss Web Server Page*

Open your downloads directory, then double-click the software package you just downloaded. Click "Agree" on the license agreement page.

Deselect components you do not want to install. Select all components, except "Abyss Web Server (32-bit)." "Start Menu Shortcuts" enables adding Abyss Web Server shortcuts in the Start Menu, and "Documentation" installs help files (Figure 1-10).

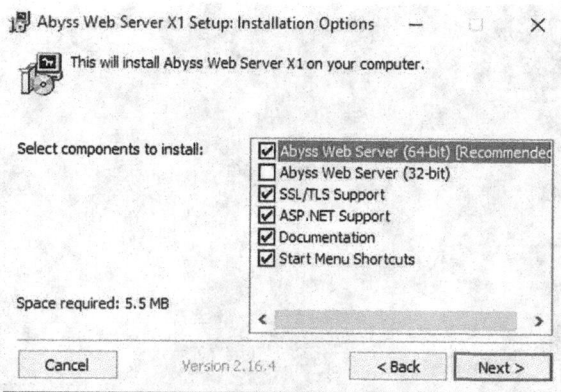

Figure 1-10. *Web Server Installation*

Choose a directory where you want to install Abyss Web Server files. Click "Install" (Figure 1-11).

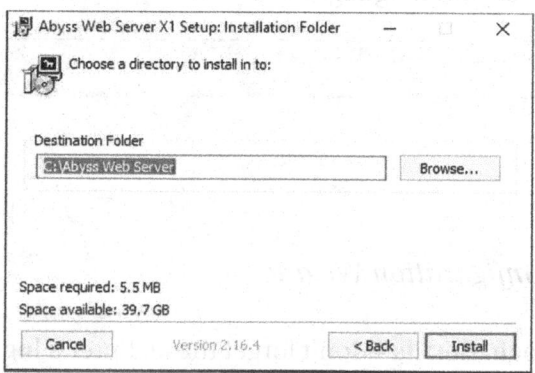

Figure 1-11. *Choose a Directory to Install the Web Server*

On your start menu, click "Abyss Web Server X1" (Figure 1-12).

Figure 1-12. *Start Menu*

The configuration wizard will appear in your web browser
(Figure 1-13). Select your language.

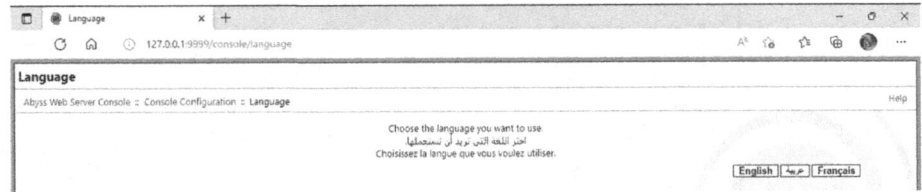

Figure 1-13. *Configuration Wizard*

Create your login details – don't forget these. Enter a login username
(e.g., admin) and a password (Figure 1-14). Click OK when you're done.

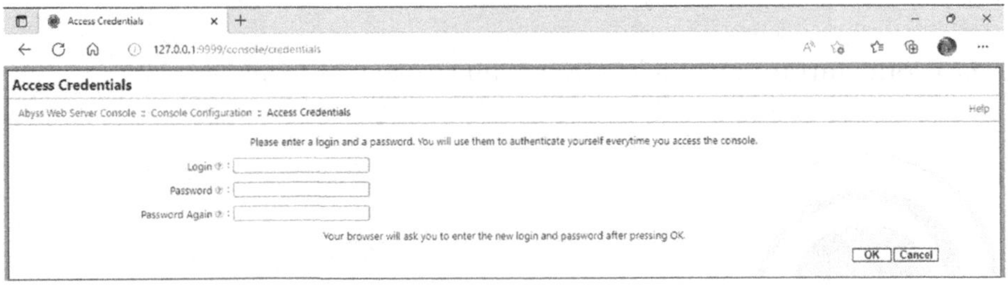

Figure 1-14. *Login Details*

When the browser asks you for a username and password, enter the username and password you chose earlier (Figure 1-15).

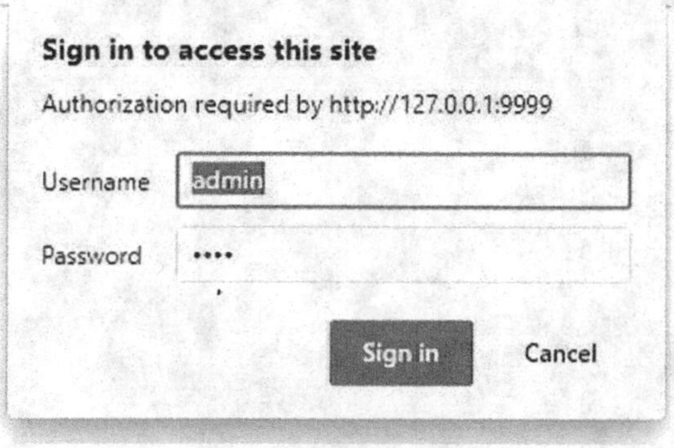

Sign in to access this site

Authorization required by http://127.0.0.1:9999

Username   admin

Password   ••••

Sign in   Cancel

Figure 1-15. *Enter Your Credentials*

Starting the Web Server

We've configured the server so it doesn't automatically start when you log in to Windows, as this could be a security risk. It is best to only run the web server when you need it to test your website.

Once the web server has been installed, you'll need to start the web server before you can do anything.

To start the server, open the start menu, then click "Abyss Web Server X1" (Figure 1-16).

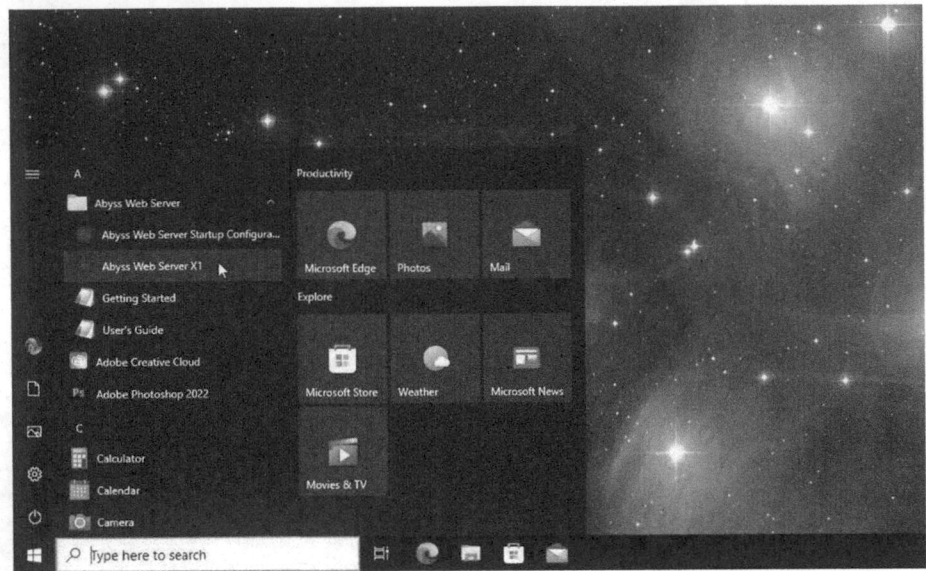

Figure 1-16. *Start Abyss Web Server*

The server will appear in the system area on the bottom right-hand side (Figure 1-17).

Figure 1-17. *Abyss Web Server in the System Area*

Saving Your Web Pages

You can save your web pages to Abyss Web Server on your local machine, or you can use FTP to upload them to a web host if you have that facility setup. In this guide, we'll save our pages to Abyss Web Server on the local machine.

Local Machine

If you have installed Abyss Web Server on your local machine, any pages you develop on your website will be saved into the following folder:

```
c:\abyss web server\htdocs
```

You'll find the folder in File Explorer on the C drive (Figure 1-18).

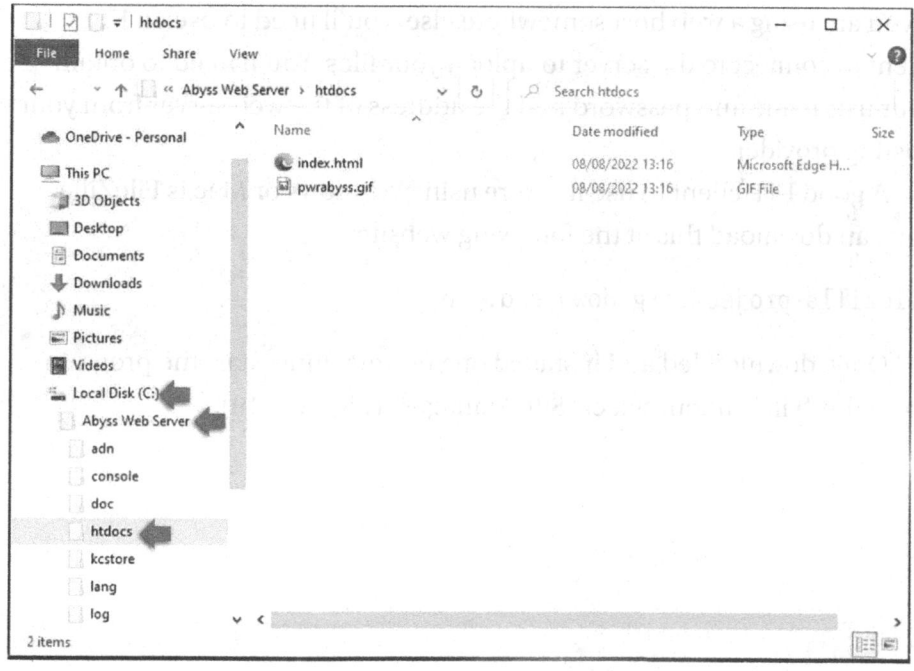

Figure 1-18. *Abyss Web Server Pages*

15

Once the server is running, you'll be able to access your web page from a web browser by navigating to

`http://localhost/`**`pagename.html`**

or

`http://127.0.0.1/`**`pagename.html`**

pagename.html is the name of the HTML document you want to view. This could be

`http://localhost/`**`index.html`**
`http://localhost/`**`store.html`**

Using a Web Host

If you are using a web host somewhere else, you'll need to use an FTP client to connect to the server to upload your files. You'll need to obtain your username and password and the address of the web server from your hosting provider.

A good FTP client to use if you're using Windows or Mac is FileZilla. You can download this at the following website:

`filezilla-project.org/download.php`

Once downloaded and installed on your machine, start the program. From the "File" menu, select "Site Manager" (Figure 1-19).

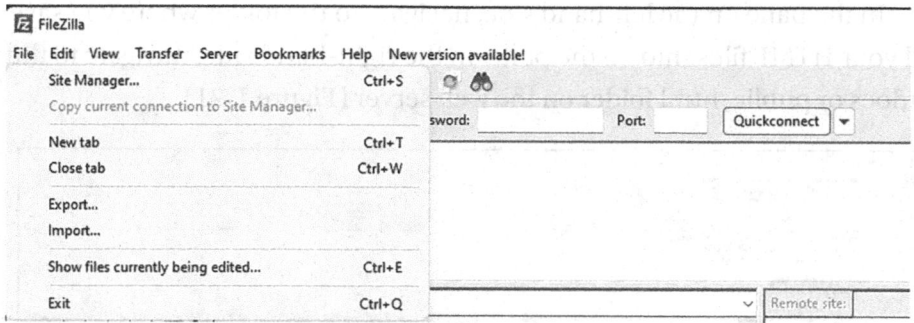

Figure 1-19. *Site Manager Using FileZilla*

Click "New site," then enter the FTP hostname or IP address, then add your username and password (Figure 1-20).

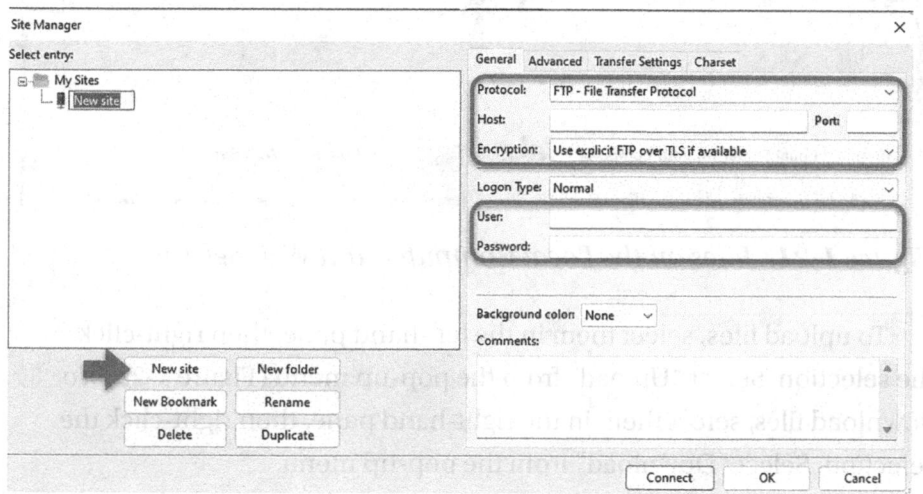

Figure 1-20. *FTP and Login Process*

Click connect to begin.

Once a connection to the server is established, you'll land on the home screen.

In the pane on the left-hand side, navigate to the folder where you save all your HTML files into. In the pane on the right-hand side, navigate to the htdocs or public_html folder on the web server (Figure 1-21).

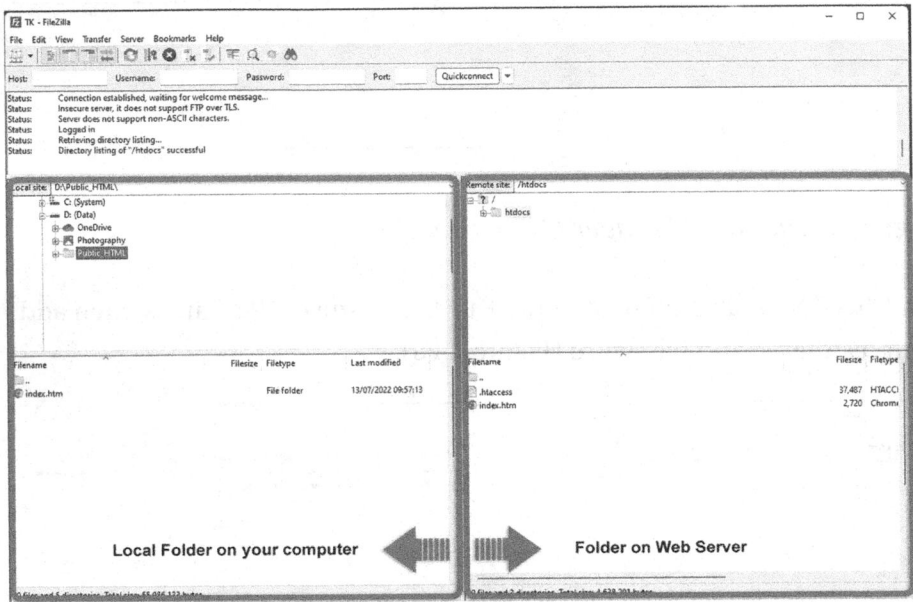

Figure 1-21. *Files on the Local Computer and Web Server*

To upload files, select them in the left-hand pane, then right-click the selection. Select "Upload" from the pop-up menu (Figure 1-22). To download files, select them in the right-hand pane, then right-click the selection. Select "Download" from the pop-up menu.

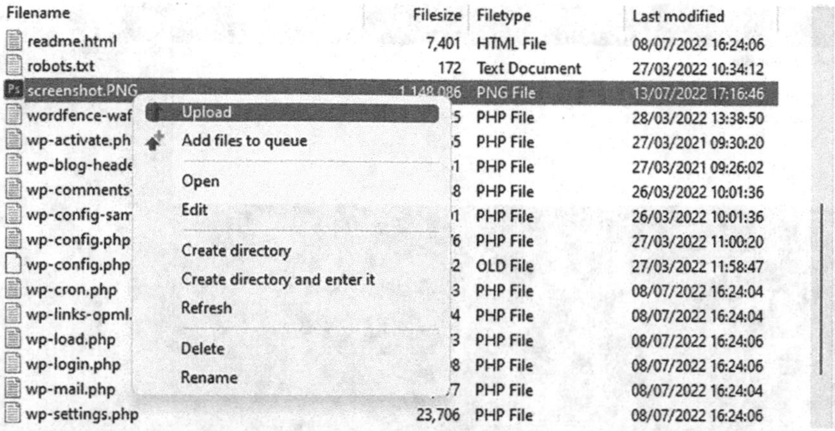

Filename	Filesize	Filetype	Last modified
readme.html	7,401	HTML File	08/07/2022 16:24:06
robots.txt	172	Text Document	27/03/2022 10:34:12
screenshot.PNG	1,148,086	PNG File	13/07/2022 17:16:46
wordfence-waf	5	PHP File	28/03/2022 13:38:50
wp-activate.ph	5	PHP File	27/03/2021 09:30:20
wp-blog-heade	1	PHP File	27/03/2021 09:26:02
wp-comments-	8	PHP File	26/03/2022 10:01:36
wp-config-sam	1	PHP File	26/03/2022 10:01:36
wp-config.php	6	PHP File	27/03/2022 11:00:20
wp-config.php	2	OLD File	27/03/2022 11:58:47
wp-cron.php	3	PHP File	08/07/2022 16:24:04
wp-links-opml.	4	PHP File	08/07/2022 16:24:04
wp-load.php	3	PHP File	08/07/2022 16:24:06
wp-login.php	8	PHP File	08/07/2022 16:24:06
wp-mail.php	7	PHP File	08/07/2022 16:24:04
wp-settings.php	23,706	PHP File	08/07/2022 16:24:06

Context menu options:
- Upload
- Add files to queue
- Open
- Edit
- Create directory
- Create directory and enter it
- Refresh
- Delete
- Rename

Figure 1-22. *Upload and Download Files*

For more detailed information on how to use FileZilla, go here:

`wiki.filezilla-project.org/Documentation`

Development Tools and Code Editors

Finding the right tool is a matter of personal preference and depends on the type of application you are going to develop. There are many different tools available. You could use an IDE which is an integrated development environment such as Adobe Dreamweaver, Brackets, or VS Code.

An IDE is a software application that consists of a source code editor with syntax highlighting to make code easier to read, as well as built-in tools to help you develop your code and a debugger to help you find errors. These are all integrated into one application, hence the name integrated development environment.

In Figure 1-23, we see Dreamweaver. You can see that it has a live preview along the top with the code underneath, with various other tools and options to help you write your code.

Figure 1-23. *Adobe Dreamweaver IDE*

Another popular IDE is Visual Studio Code or VS Code for short. You can download VS Code from the following website:

`code.visualstudio.com`

In Figure 1-24, we can see VS Code on the left-hand side showing our HTML code with a browser preview open on the right showing the output of the HTML code.

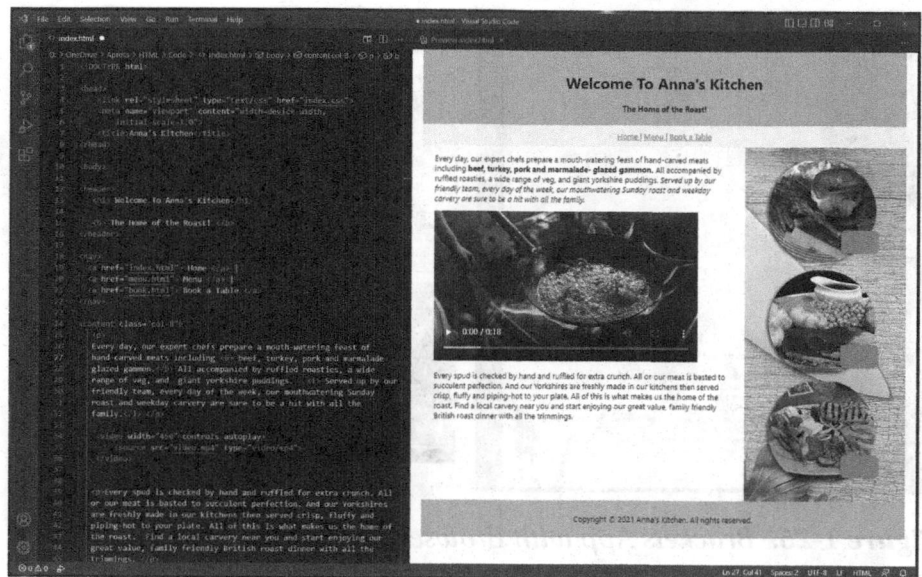

Figure 1-24. *VS Code IDE*

Another code editor to try is Brackets. Brackets is a free editor that you can download from the developer's website:

`www.brackets.io`

In Figure 1-25, you can see the Brackets window open on the left-hand side, and it makes quite a nice little editor for coding. On the right-hand side, you can open up your live preview to see what your page looks like as you're writing your code.

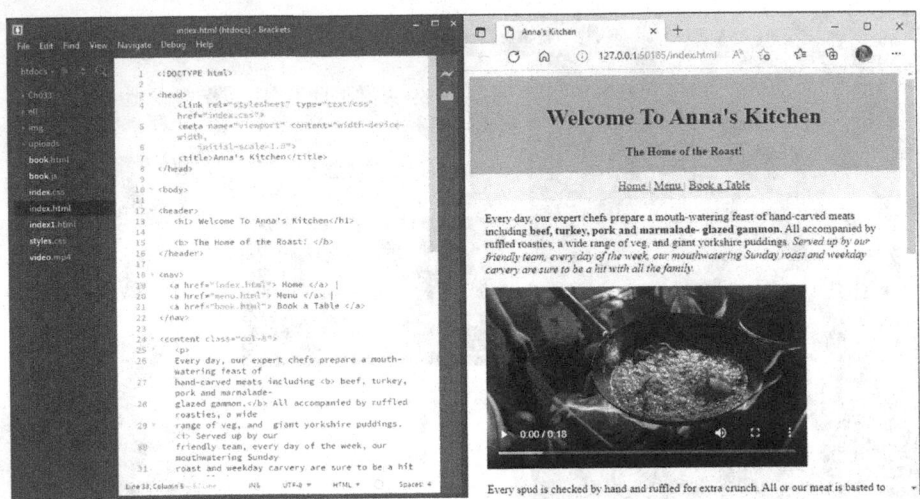

Figure 1-25. *Brackets App with Browser Preview*

You can use any of these tools to write your code. Some of these IDEs can be quite complex, so while you are learning, I suggest you stick with Notepad and write the code manually so you can understand the structure and meaning without distractions.

Throughout this book, we'll be using Notepad/TextEdit to write our code as shown in Figure 1-26; however, you can use any code editor you like such as VS Code if you prefer.

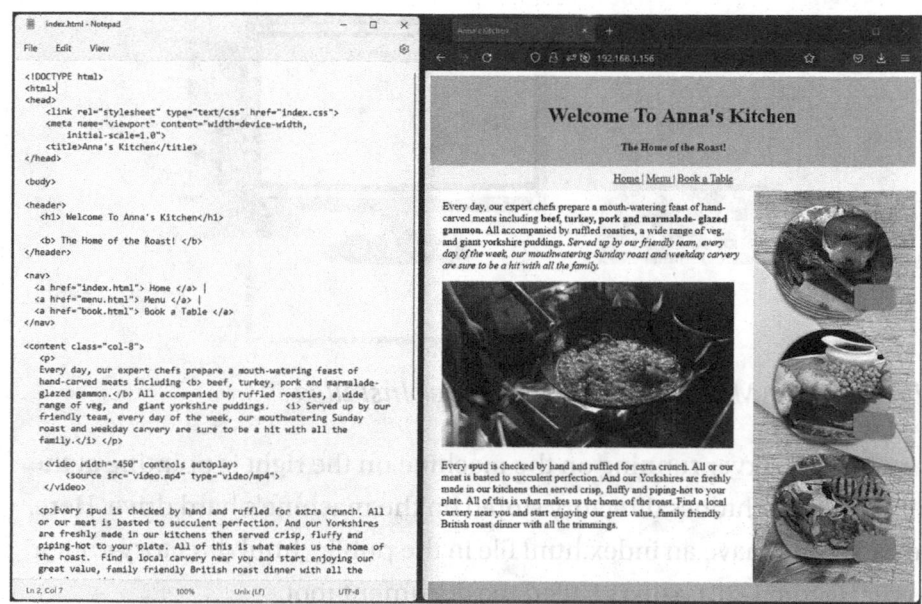

Figure 1-26. *Notepad Code Editor and Browser Preview*

Lab Demo

In this demo, we're going to explore how web servers work.

In Figure 1-27, the machine on the right has our web server installed. A web server is a program that runs on the machine and serves web pages (such as Abyss that we installed earlier). The web server software is bound to a port. A port is a number used to identify a service running on a machine. In this case, the service is a web server and is bound to port 80. This machine is connected to a small network using cat5 cables through a network switch.

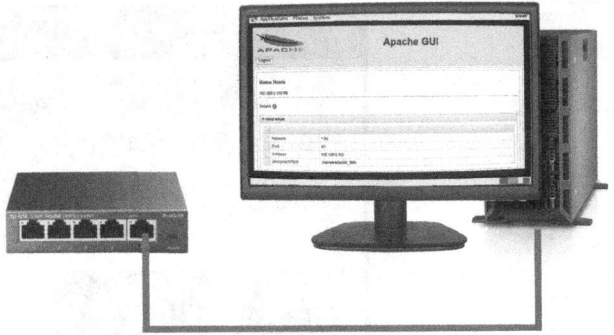

Figure 1-27. *Machine with Web Server Installed*

The web server running on the machine on the right is pointing at the public_html or htdocs directory stored on the machine's hard drive. Here, we can see we have an index.html file in the public_html directory on our server (Figure 1-28). This is called the document root.

Figure 1-28. *Document Root*

Each computer on the network has an IP address, which is an address that uniquely identifies a device on a network. The web server has an IP address of 192.168.0.100 and is bound to port 80 (the default for unencrypted web traffic). You can see the configuration summary as follows:

- IP address: 192.168.0.100

- Port: 80

- Document root: /var/www/public_html

Let's add another computer. The computer on the left is called a client and is a laptop running Windows with a web browser installed (Figure 1-29). The browser could be Edge, Firefox, or Chrome.

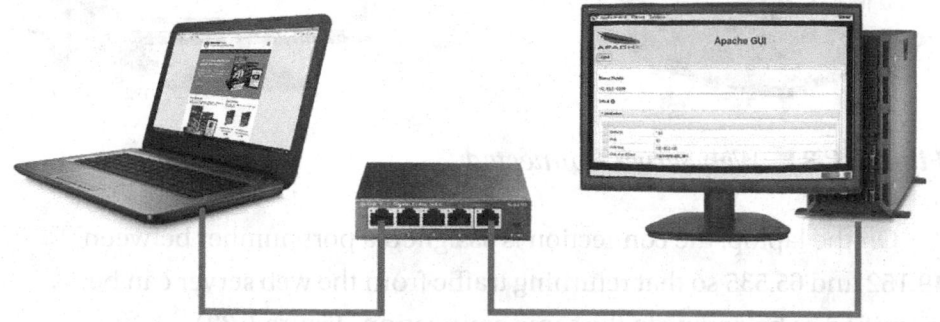

Figure 1-29. *Client Accessing a Web Server*

This laptop connects to the web server using the IP address allocated to the machine running the web server. On the laptop, we can type this IP address into the address bar at the top of the browser: 192.168.0.100 (Figure 1-30).

Figure 1-30. *IP Address*

The laptop will connect to the web server using the server's IP address through port 80 (Figure 1-31).

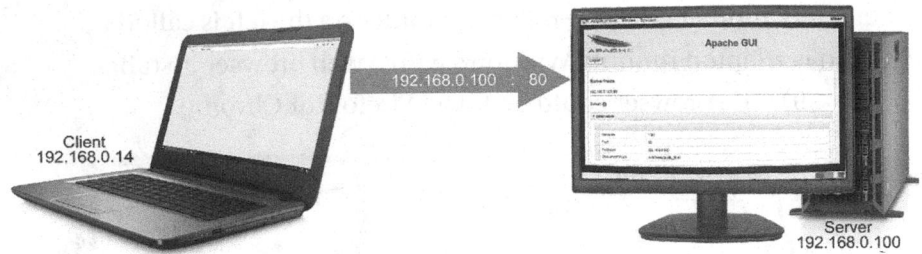

Figure 1-31. *Web Server Connected*

On the laptop, the connection is assigned a port number between 49,152 and 65,535 so that returning traffic from the web server can be identified as belonging to the same connection (Figure 1-32).

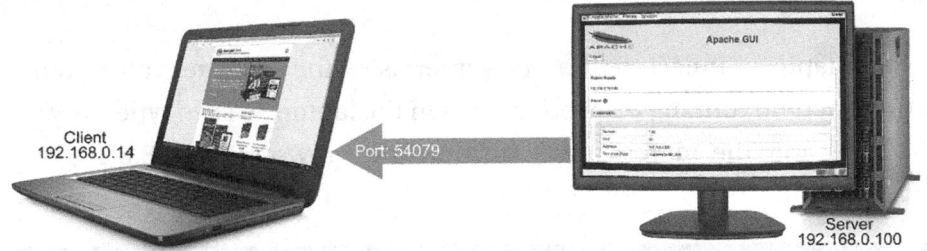

Figure 1-32. *Connection Assigned Port Number*

The IP address and the port number form a socket. There will be a socket on the server and one on the laptop (client). Each socket is unique and bidirectional, so applications can send and receive data (Figure 1-33).

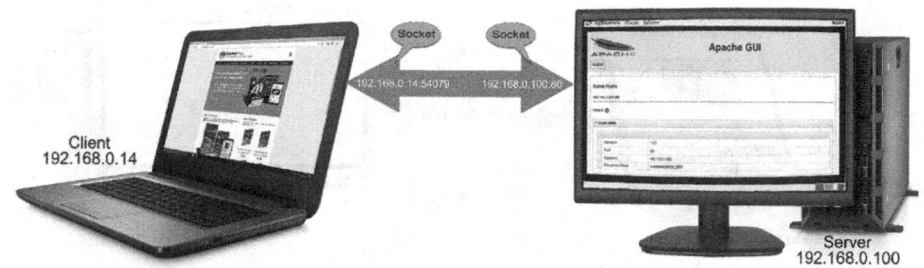

Figure 1-33. *Socket*

Once a connection is established, the web server reads the index HTML file in the public_html directory and sends the code in this file to the laptop (client).

The browser on the laptop (client) then reads the HTML code and creates the web page you see on your screen.

You may have noticed that when visiting a website, you don't type in a string of numbers, you type in a domain name. The problem is computers don't understand domain names, only IP addresses, so we need to convert them.

In order to do this, we need to add another server to the mix called a DNS server. This server converts our memorable domain names into IP addresses.

When you enter the domain name into your browser, for example, elluminetpress.com, your computer (the laptop) will send the domain name to a DNS server. The DNS server responds with the IP address (e.g., 192.168.0.100) (Figure 1-34).

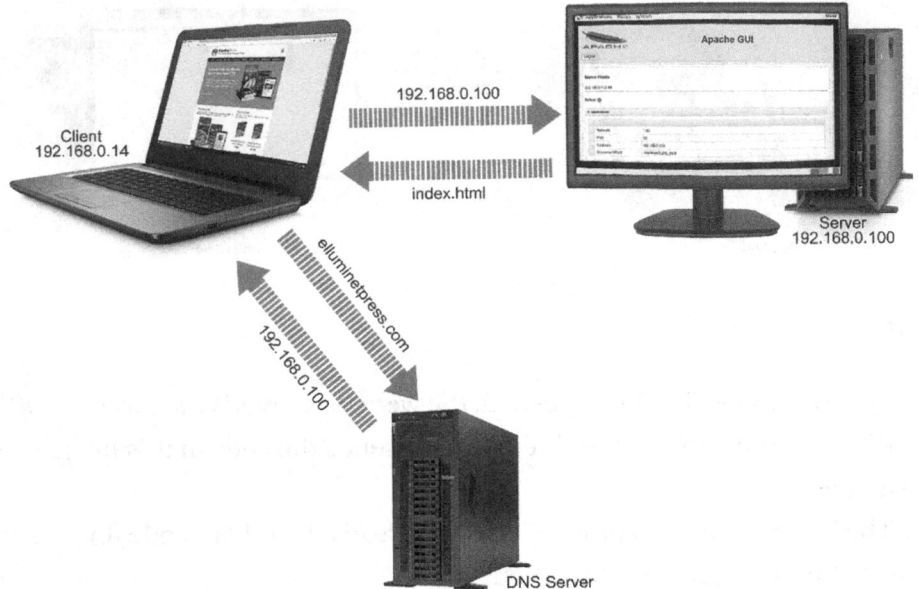

Figure 1-34. *Computer Connecting to the Web Server*

Your computer (i.e., the laptop) then uses this IP address to connect to the web server as before.

Lab Exercises

1. Set up your personal web server on your computer or get access to a web host to host your HTML files.

2. Choose a text editor to edit your code, for example, Notepad.

3. What is hypertext?

4. What is a URL?

5. What is HTML?

6. What is CSS?

7. What is a web server?

8. What is the purpose of an index.html file?

9. What is an IP address?

10. What is the purpose of a DNS server?

Summary

- Web pages are all linked together using clickable text or images, called hyperlinks.

- Code editors and IDEs

  - VS Code

  - Dreamweaver

  - Brackets

  - Text editor (Notepad, TextEdit, etc.)

- A website and its pages are stored or hosted on a web server.

- A DNS server translates domain names into IP addresses.

- An IP address is a unique address that identifies a device on the Internet.

CHAPTER 2

Introduction to HTML

In this chapter, we'll take a look at the basics of an HTML document. The basic structure of an HTML document has three parts:

- Document type declaration at the top
- Document header
- Body

Structure of an HTML Page

We can see in Figure 2-1 that an HTML page is a text file containing the elements and information the web browser uses to display the web page. Static web pages have the file extension **.htm** or more commonly **.html**.

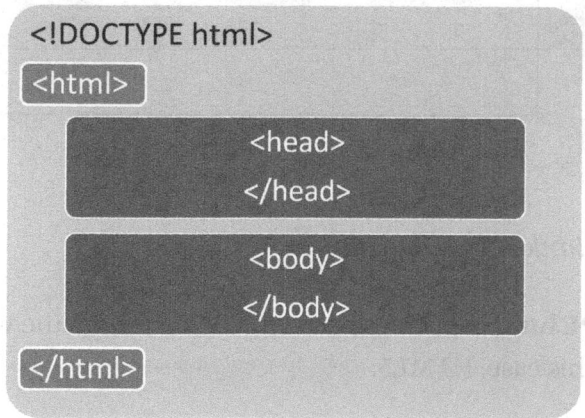

Figure 2-1. *Structure of an HTML Document*

© Kevin Wilson 2023
K. Wilson, *The Absolute Beginner's Guide to HTML and CSS*,
https://doi.org/10.1007/978-1-4842-9250-1_2

At the top on the first line, we have the document type declaration.

Underneath, we have the first <html> element. This defines the start of the HTML page.

Inside the <html> elements, we have the <head> element. This contains information about the page as well as the document title.

Underneath, we have the <body> element. This is where the main body of the document is defined. This is the bit you see in your browser window.

Finally, we need to close the <html> element. This marks the end of the document.

Let's explore an example in a bit more detail. Here, you can see a simplified web page broken down to its most basic elements (Figure 2-2).

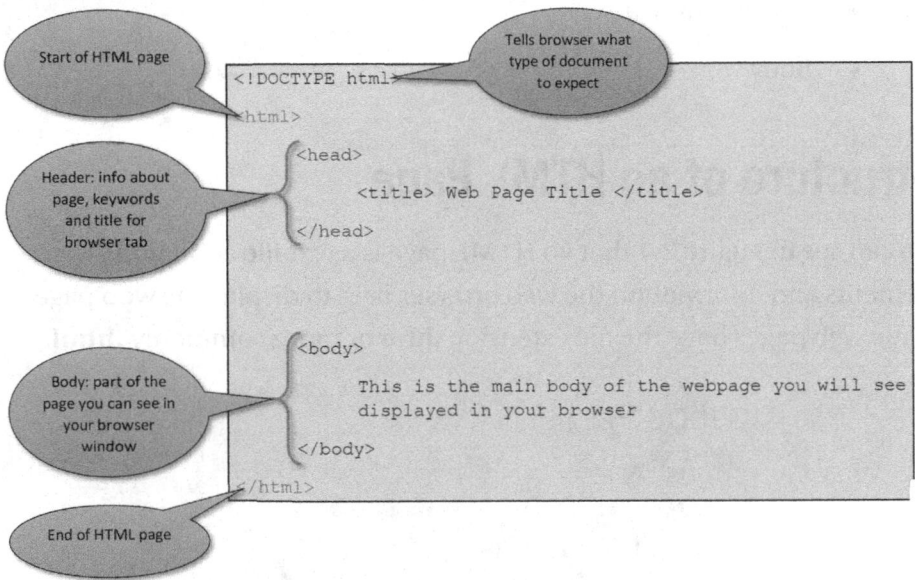

Figure 2-2. *Blank HTML Document*

<!DOCTYPE html> specifies what type of document the web browser can expect, in this case, HTML5.

The **<html>** element contains all the HTML code and defines the start of the HTML page. You can also specify the language by adding the lang attribute:

> <html **lang="en"**> to specify English
>
> <html **lang="es"**> to specify Spanish
>
> <html **lang="fr"**> to specify French
>
> <html **lang="de"**> to specify German

In the **<head>** of the document, you'll find

> **<title>**: This is where we insert the page name as it will appear at the top of the browser window or tab.
>
> **<style>**: This is where you define embedded style information for an HTML document using CSS. See Chapter 4.
>
> **<link>**: Link to an external style sheet. See Chapter 4.
>
> **<script>**: This is used to define client-side scripts, such as JavaScript. See Chapter 8.
>
> **<meta>**: This is where information about the document is stored – character encoding, name, description, etc. See the "Metadata" section later in this chapter.

The **<body>** element contains all the elements and is where the main content is written to display on the web page.

You might also find the following elements:

> **<!-- ... -->**

These elements specify a comment for the developer's benefit and are ignored by the browser. Comments are useful to document your code and explain its function.

HTML Element Structure

Technically, an HTML element consists of a start tag, the element's attributes, the visible bit or the content, and an end tag. The HTML tag is used to mark the start or end of an element.

Let's take a closer look at how HTML elements are constructed. Elements start with an opening tag and end with a closing tag. The tags themselves start and end with angle brackets < >.

In the example in Figure 2-3, let's have a look at the anchor element. This element creates a hyperlink to another web page. The HTML element starts with an opening tag and ends with a closing tag.

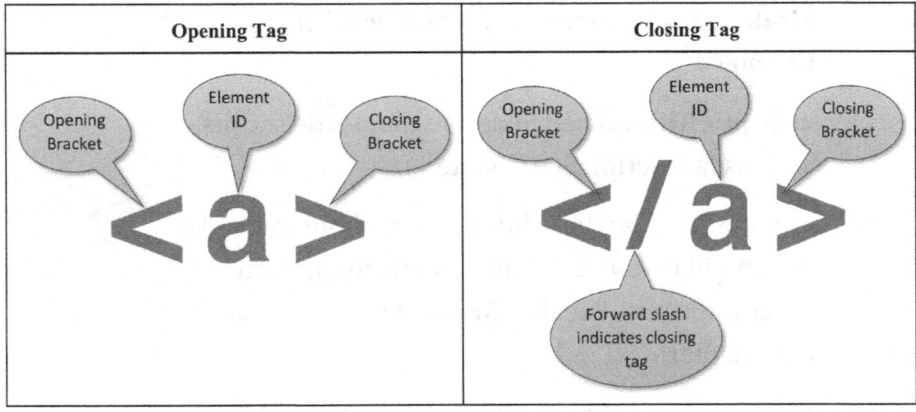

Figure 2-3. *HTML Opening and Closing Tags*

The bit visible to the user goes in between the two tags.

The opening HTML tag often contains some attributes that define the HTML element's properties and are used to control formatting, size, page link references, and so on, and it is placed inside the element's opening tag. For example, see Figure 2-4.

<a href="about.html">
‾‾ ‾‾‾‾‾‾‾‾ ‾‾‾‾‾‾‾‾‾‾‾
Element ID   Attribute   Attribute Value

Figure 2-4. *HTML Tag Structure*

HTML attributes are made up of two parts: a name and a value.

- The **name** is the attribute you want to set. For example, the anchor <a> element contains an attribute named "href," which indicates the address of the page you want to link to.

- The **value** is what you want the attribute to be set to and is always contained within quotation marks. In this example, the page we want to link to is called "about.html".

Let's take a look at an example. Here, we want to add the link "about us" to a website. The anchor element is represented by "a" and is written as

```
<a href = "about.html"> About Us </a>
```

Let's break the element down and see how it works.

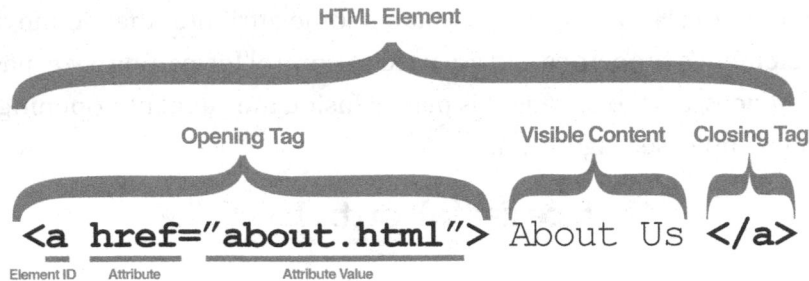

Figure 2-5. *An HTML Element*

The element starts with an opening angle bracket <, followed by the element ID of the element we want to use, in this case, the "a" for anchor. After that, we add any attributes as we can see in Figure 2-5.

Attributes contain additional pieces of information. Attributes take the form of an opening tag, and additional info is placed inside. For example, in the HTML tag earlier, "href" is an attribute, and "about.html" is the value of the attribute.

We close the opening tag with an angle bracket >.

After the opening tag, we add the visible bit that the user will see on the web page "About Us."

The closing tag contains a forward slash before the element ID, in this case:

```
</a>
```

In Figure 2-6, we can see the anchor element in the HTML document on the left. The text "About Us" appears on the web page in the browser window and is linked to the page about.html.

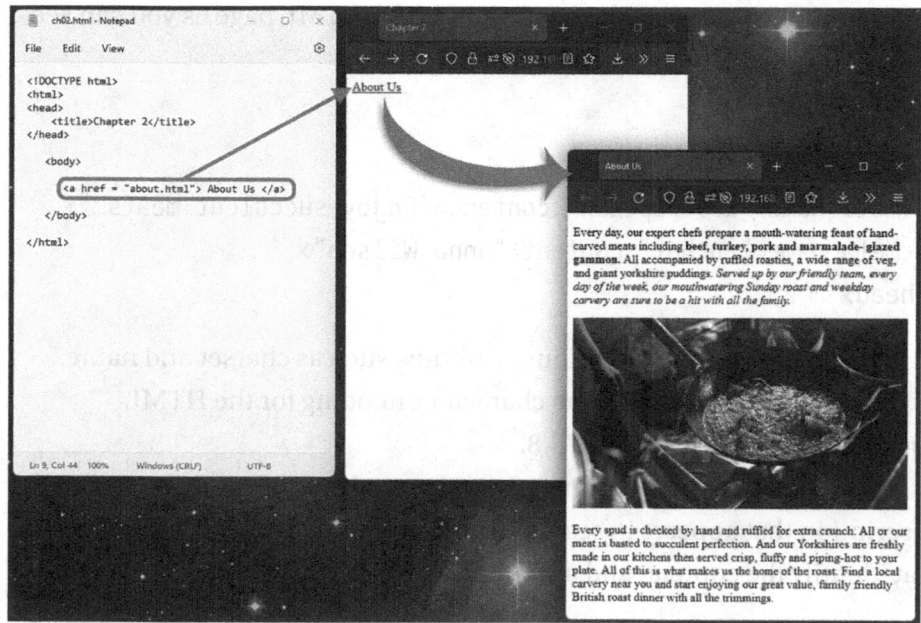

Figure 2-6. *Anchor Element*

Similarly with an image element, we start with the opening <img> tag, then add the src attribute containing the image we want to display:

```
<img src="profilepic.jpg">
```

The image source (src) is an attribute of the opening <img> tag. Notice that the <img> element doesn't have a closing tag. This is known as an empty, self-closing, or void element.

Metadata

Metadata is additional information about an HTML document. The meta elements can be used to describe properties of the HTML document, such as author, date, and content descriptions. Metadata is used by browsers to determine how to display content and by search engines such as Bing or Google to work out what a web page is about.

<meta> always go inside the <head> of the HTML page as you can see in the following:

```
<head>
  <meta charset="UTF-8">
  <meta name="description" content="Enjoy succulent meats…">
  <meta name="author" content="Anna Wilson">
</head>
```

The meta element has various attributes such as charset and name.

A meta charset specifies the character encoding for the HTML document which is usually UTF-8.

A meta name specifies names for the metadata such as a content description that appears in search engine results of the page, keywords that identify the content, and author of the page.

Lab Exercises

1. Open a new text file and save it as ch02.html.

2. Write the basic structure of an HTML document.

3. What is an HTML tag?

4. What is an HTML element?

5. What's the difference between an HTML tag and an HTML element?

6. What is metadata?

7. What is the <head> section for in an HTML document? What other elements can you include?

Summary

- An HTML element consists of a start tag, the element's attributes, the visible bit or the content, and an end tag. The HTML tag is used to mark the start or end of an element.

- <!DOCTYPE html> specifies what type of document the web browser can expect, in this case, HTML5.

- Head elements contain information about the page as well as the document title. These also contain other elements such as title to specify a page title for the browser window, style to include CSS styles, script to include any JavaScripts, and meta to include metadata.

- The body elements contain the main body of the document. This is the bit you see in your browser window.

CHAPTER 3

Getting Started with HTML

In this chapter, we are going to build a very simple home page for our restaurant website using common text formatting elements, and we'll add some images, links, tables, and lists.

This will provide you with a foundation and basic structure of a web page using HTML, which you can build on later.

We'll walk through the process from a blank HTML document, then build the home page using the HTML elements.

We'll also look at how to use the style attributes of each HTML element. You can apply styles directly in the HTML code each time you want to use the style such as fonts, text color, and page color. This, however, is a bit cumbersome and becomes very difficult to maintain in the long run, especially in larger projects where there is a lot of code. A much better way is to use a style sheet or CSS to set fonts, text color, and page color. This allows you to define all your styles once and in one place, usually in a styles.css file. You can then call the CSS file from within your HTML code, which we'll look at in the next chapter.

For now, let's concentrate on HTML code.

© Kevin Wilson 2023
K. Wilson, *The Absolute Beginner's Guide to HTML and CSS*,
https://doi.org/10.1007/978-1-4842-9250-1_3

Setting Up

For the exercises in this chapter, we will be using Notepad and a web browser. We'll be saving our HTML files into the htdocs folder on our personal web server we installed in Chapter 1.

Open your text editor. I'm going to use Notepad. This is where we're going to type in our code. We're going to start with the outline of an HTML document. For example, see Figure 3-1.

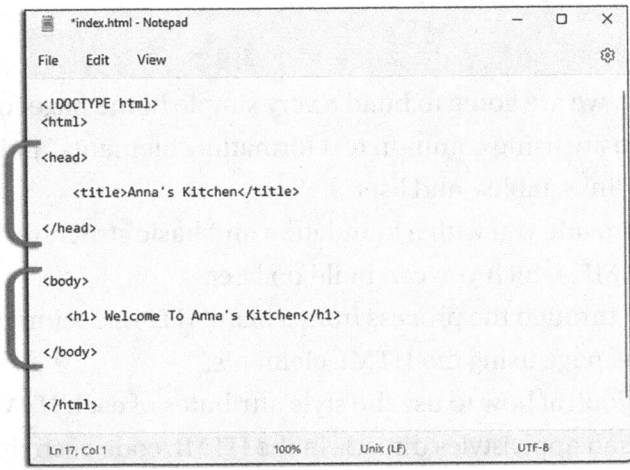

Figure 3-1. *HTML Document Outline*

To save the file, go to the "File" menu, then click "Save as" (Figure 3-2).

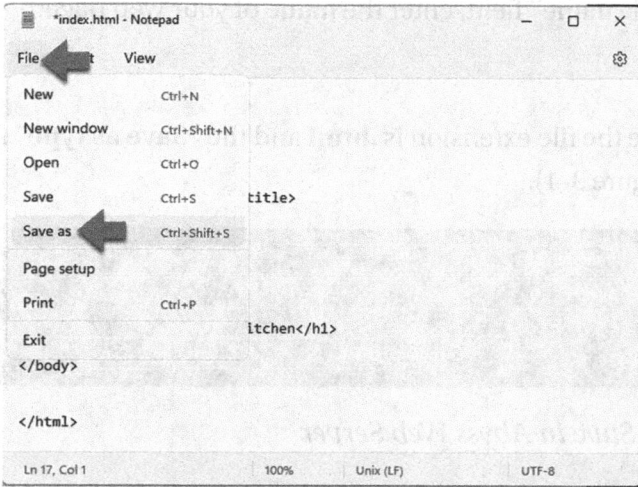

Figure 3-2. *Save As in Notepad*

From the "Save As" dialog box, navigate to your "Abyss Web Server" folder on the C drive, then select "htdocs" (Figure 3-3).

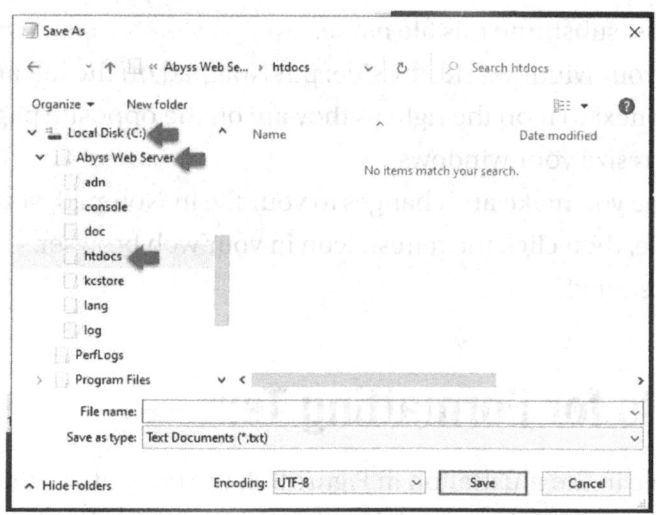

Figure 3-3. *Save in Abyss Web Server*

In the "File name" field, enter the name of your web page:

`index.html`

Make sure the file extension is **.html** and the "**Save as type**" is set to "All files" (Figure 3-4).

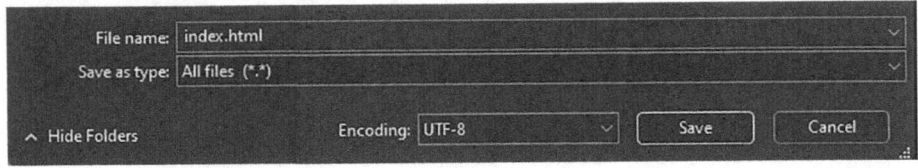

Figure 3-4. *Save in Abyss Web Server*

With the Abyss Personal Web Server running, open your web browser. Enter the following into the address bar at the top:

`http://127.0.0.1/index.html`

index.html is the file we want to view. To view any other HTML files you create, just substitute this file name.

Arrange your windows side by side; put Notepad on the left and your web browser next to it on the right as they are on the opposite page. You may need to resize your windows.

Every time you make any changes to your file in Notepad, you'll need to save the file, then click the refresh icon in your web browser.

Let's get started.

Elements for Formatting Text

As you can see in the illustration in Figure 3-5, the text in the <title> tags appears on the title tab in the web browser, and anything between the <body> tags appears in the browser window.

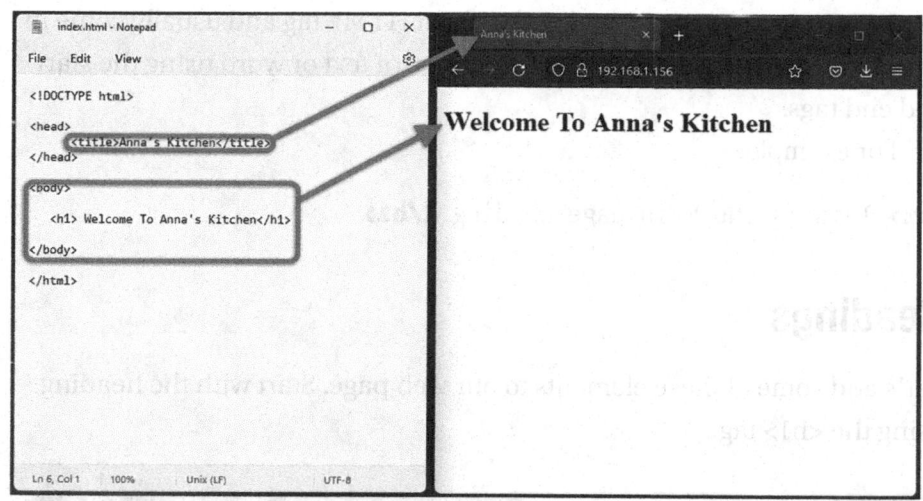

Figure 3-5. *Title and Body Text*

HTML elements label the pieces of your web page, such as headings, text formatting with bold or italic, paragraphs, images, links, and tables.

Let's have a look at some simple formatting elements.

Main Heading Style

```
<h1>...</h1>
```

Subheading Style

```
<h2>...</h2>
```

Bold Text

```
<b>...</b>
```

Italic Text

```
<i>...</i>
```

Paragraph Text

```
<p>...</p>
```

45

HTML elements begin and end with an HTML tag and usually come in pairs, and you'll need to surround the piece of text or word using the start and end tags.

For example:

`<h1>` `This is the main page heading` **`</h1>`**

Headings

Let's add some of these elements to our web page. Start with the heading, using the <h1> tag.

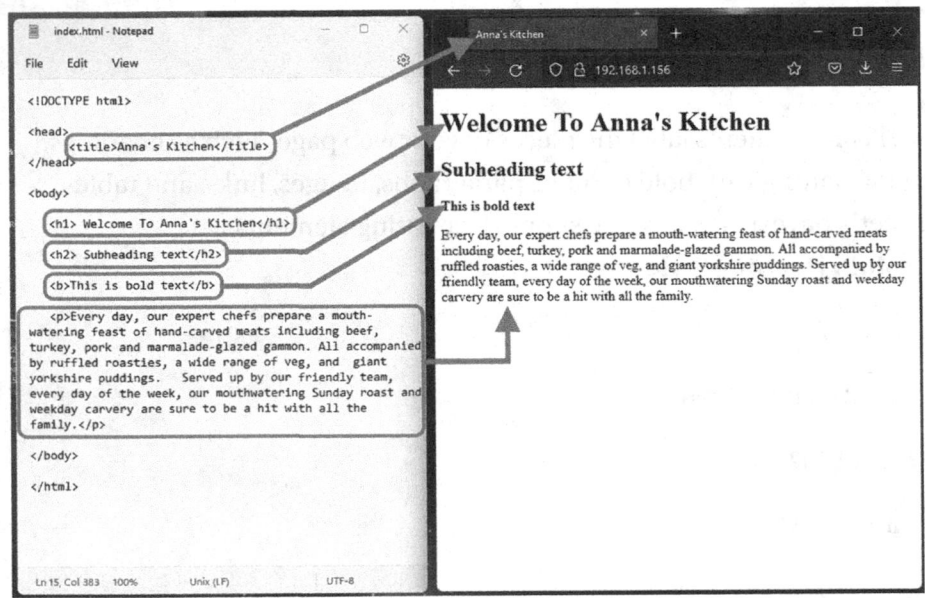

Figure 3-6. *HTML Text Editor*

In the illustration in Figure 3-6, the HTML document is open in a text editor on the left. The same document is open in a web browser on the right, and you can see the effect that each element has on the text, as indicated by the red arrows.

Browsers do not display the HTML elements but use them to format the content of the page according to their function.

Paragraphs

You can also add paragraphs. It is best practice to add all your paragraphs between <p>...</p> tags:

<p> Every day, our expert chefs prepare a mouth-watering feast of hand-carved meats including beef, turkey, pork and marmalade-glazed gammon. All accompanied by ruffled roasties, a wide range of veg, and giant yorkshire puddings.   Served up by our friendly team, every day of the week, our mouthwatering Sunday roast and weekday carvery are sure to be a hit with all the family.**</p>**

Bold Text

You can also make text bold or strong. Just surround the word or words with the tags:

**** beef, turkey, pork and marmalade-glazed gammon****
**** beef, turkey, pork and marmalade-glazed gammon ****

Have a look at the example (Figure 3-7).

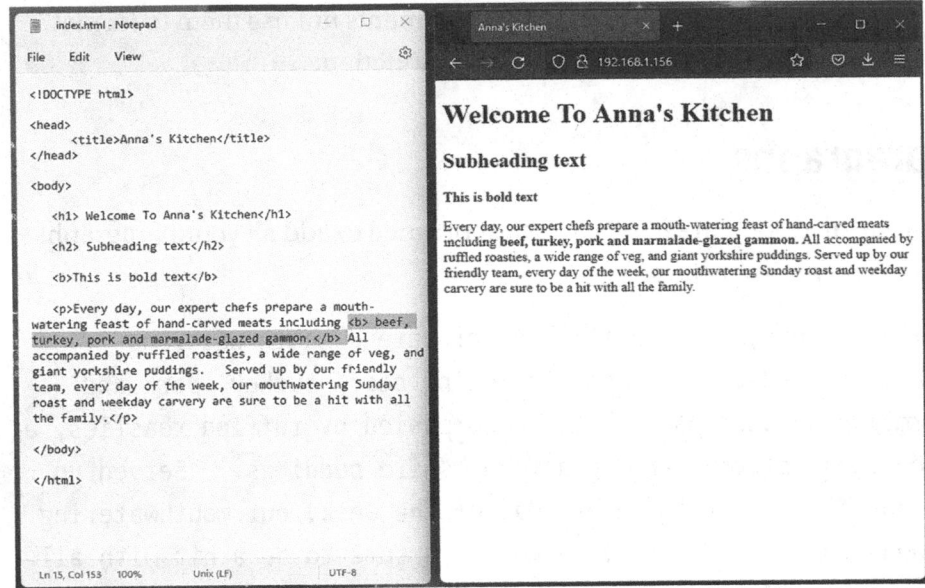

Figure 3-7. *Bold Text*

The text "**beef, turkey, pork and marmalade-glazed gammon.**" appears in bold or strong text.

Italic Text

You can also make text italic or emphasized. The <i> tag marks text in an alternate voice, and the content inside is usually displayed in italic type. The <em> tag marks text as emphasized, and the content inside is usually displayed in italic type.

To use these tags, just surround the word or words with the <i> or <em> tags:

```
<i> Served up by our friendly team, every day of the week, our
mouthwatering Sunday roast and weekday carvery are sure to be a
hit with all the family. </i>
```

**** Served up by our friendly team, every day of the week, our mouthwatering Sunday roast and weekday carvery are sure to be a hit with all the family. ****

Have a look at the example (Figure 3-8). The text "*Served up by our friendly team, every day of the week, our mouthwatering Sunday roast and weekday carvery are sure to be a hit with all the family*" appears in italic or emphasized text.

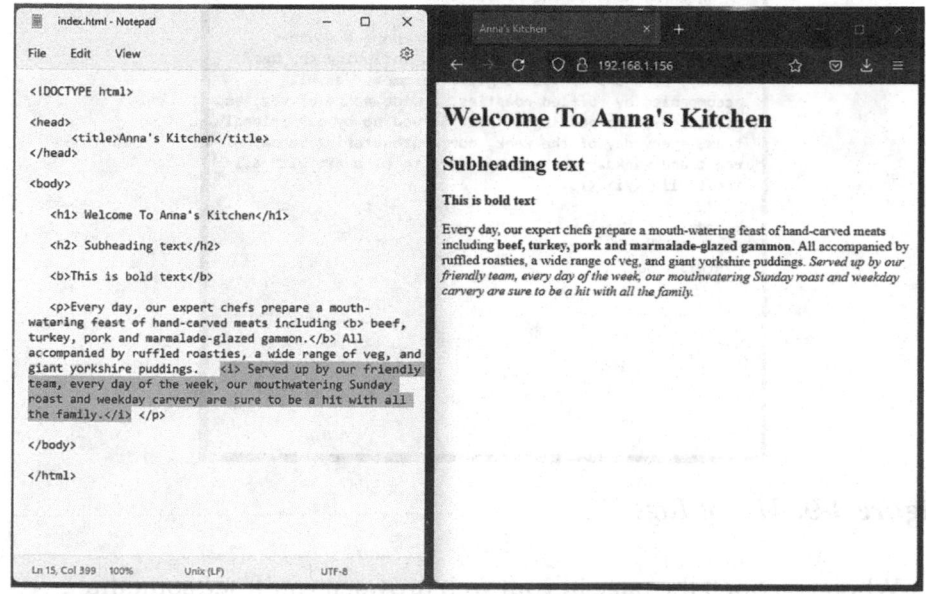

Figure 3-8. *Italics*

Now let's put it all together using the information we just learned. In the body of your HTML document, try adding the example in Figure 3-9.

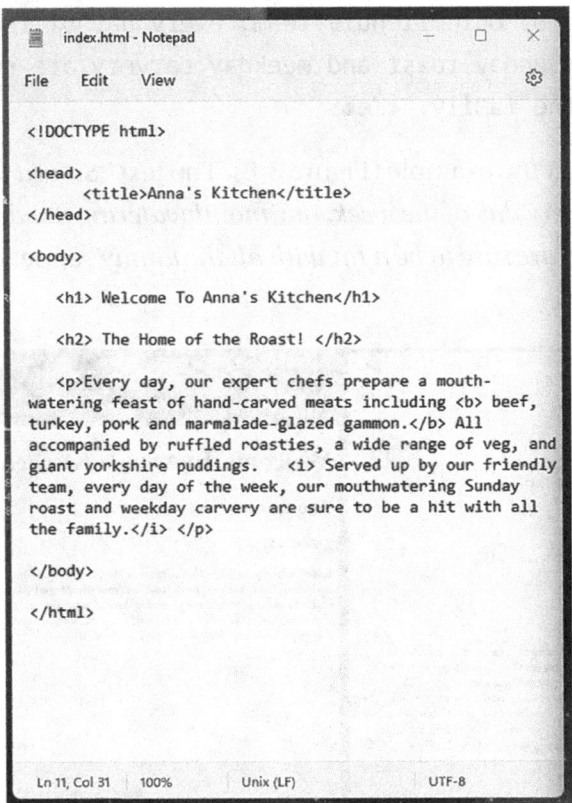

Figure 3-9. *Use of Tags*

When you open the page in your web browser, you'll see something like Figure 3-10.

Figure 3-10. *Tags in Use*

The heading has been rendered using <H1>, and the tag line has been rendered in bold text using <b>.

Also, we have created a paragraph using the <p> tags. This tag splits the text into neatly spaced paragraphs.

Page Background Color

To change the background color on any object, add the style attribute. Set it to "background-color" and then choose a color from the HTML color list:

```
<body style = "background-color:Orange;">
```

Have a look at the code in Figure 3-11.

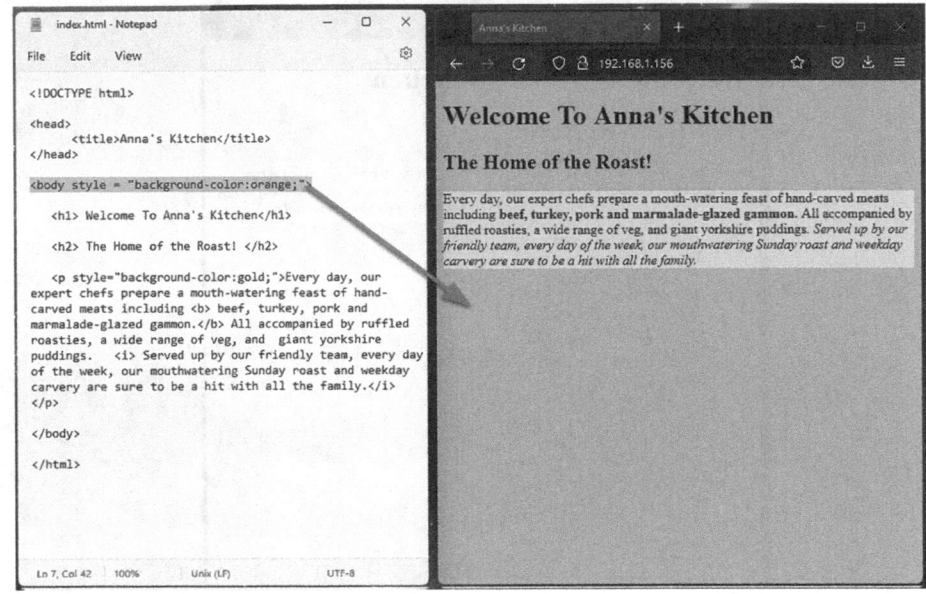

Figure 3-11. *Background Color*

You can also change the background color of other objects, such as the paragraph background (Figure 3-12):

```
<p style = "background-color:Gold">
```

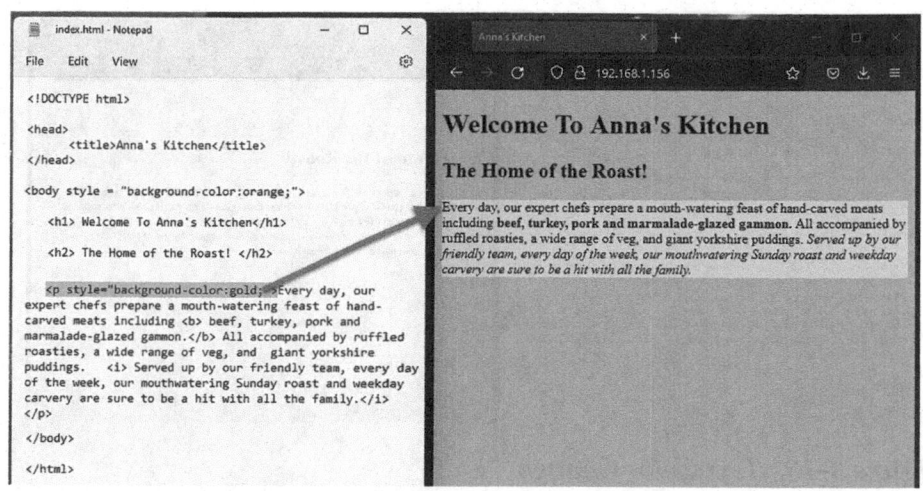

Figure 3-12. *Background Color of Objects*

Text Color

To change the text color, add the style attribute to a style (Figure 3-13). Set the attribute to "color" and then select a color from the list of HTML colors:

```
<H1 style = "color:Yellow;">
```

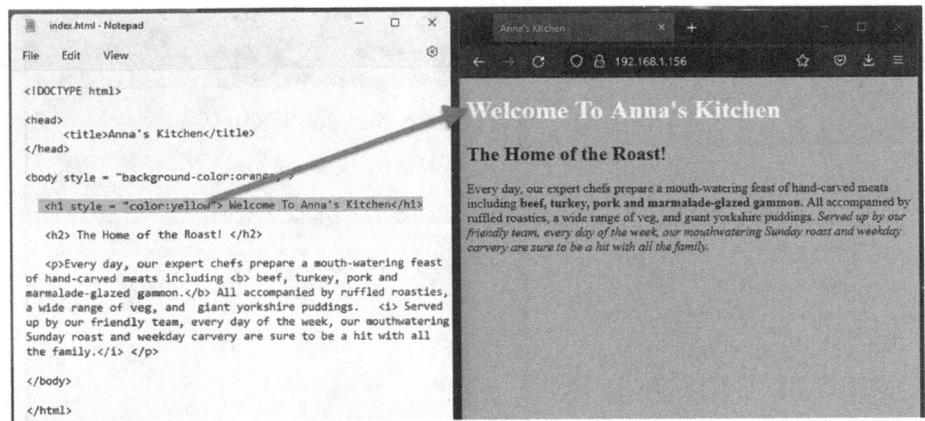

Figure 3-13. *Text Color Change*

Fonts

To change the font, add the style attribute to a style. Set the attribute font-family to the font name you want (Figure 3-14). In this example, I'm using Helvetica:

```
<h2 style = "font-family:Helvetica;">The Home of the
Roast!</h2>
```

Let's add this line to our HTML file.

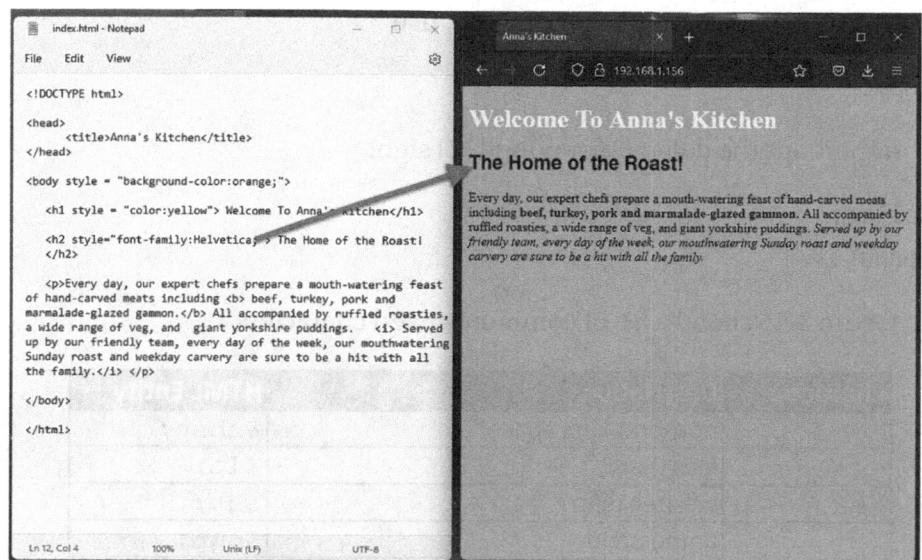

Figure 3-14. *Changing the Font*

The font on the subheading has changed to Helvetica.

You can choose from a variety of fonts. Not all of them are supported by all browsers but most of them are.

You can also make use of Google Fonts.

HTML Entities

An HTML entity is a bit of text that begins with an ampersand and ends with a semicolon and is frequently used to display reserved characters which would otherwise be interpreted as HTML code, invisible characters such as nonbreaking spaces, and symbols. A commonly used entity in HTML is the nonbreaking space:

` `

If you want to add the copyright sign, use

©

or perhaps the dollar ($) or pound (£) sign:

$
£

Figure 3-15 shows a list of commonly used characters.

Character	Description	HTML Entity
	non-breaking space	
<	less than	&lt;
>	greater than	&gt;
&	ampersand	&amp;
"	double quotation mark	&quot;
'	single quotation mark (apostrophe)	&apos;
¢	cent	&cent;
£	pound	&pound;
¥	yen	&yen;
€	euro	&euro;
©	copyright	&copy;
®	registered trademark	&reg;

Figure 3-15. *Commonly Used Characters*

Adding Images

To add an image, use the <img> element:

```
<img src = "img/carvery.jpg" width=" " height=" ">
```

Use the src attribute to specify the file name and location of the image. It is advised to keep images in a separate folder called "img," "images," or sometimes "assets." This helps to keep all your files organized. In this guide, we'll save our images into the "img" folder on our web server.

To reference the image in the src attribute of the img element, add the folder name followed by a forward slash, then the image name (Figure 3-16).

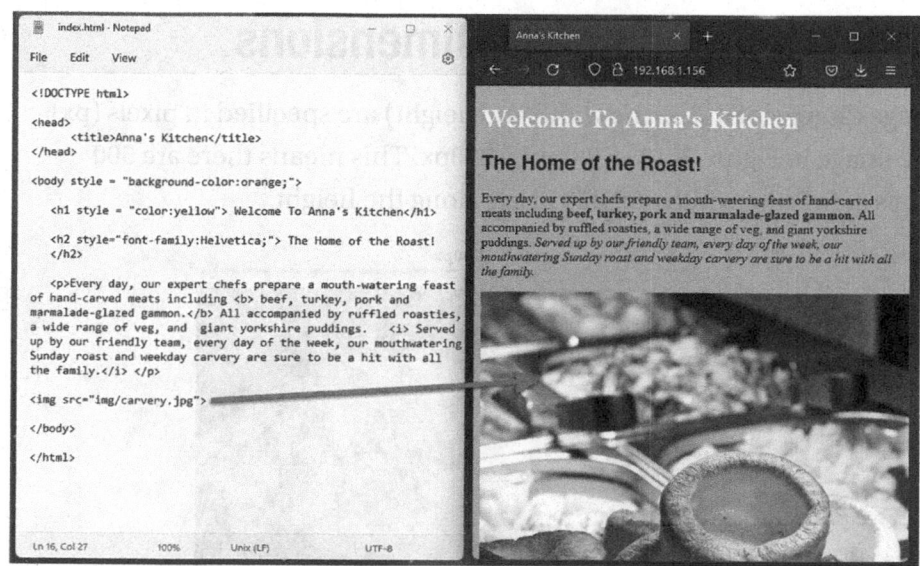

Figure 3-16. *Adding an Image*

Notice that the size of this image is large. You can also specify the size of the image using the width and height attributes measured in pixels (px).

Figure 3-17. *Image Size*

By default, the image will be displayed according to the saved width and height of the actual image (Figure 3-17), but you can override this.

Understanding Image Dimensions

Image dimensions (i.e., the width and height) are specified in pixels (px). The image in Figure 3-18 is 500px by 220px. This means there are 500 pixels across the width and 220 pixels along the height.

Figure 3-18. *Image Resizing*

If you look at the image in Figure 3-18, it is a bit small and could do with expanding to the length of the page.

The width of 500px would be a better fit, so add the width attribute and set it to "500" (Figure 3-19):

```
<img src="img/carvery.jpg" width="500">
```

This will widen the image and automatically adjust the length to prevent the image from being stretched.

You can also specify both width and height.

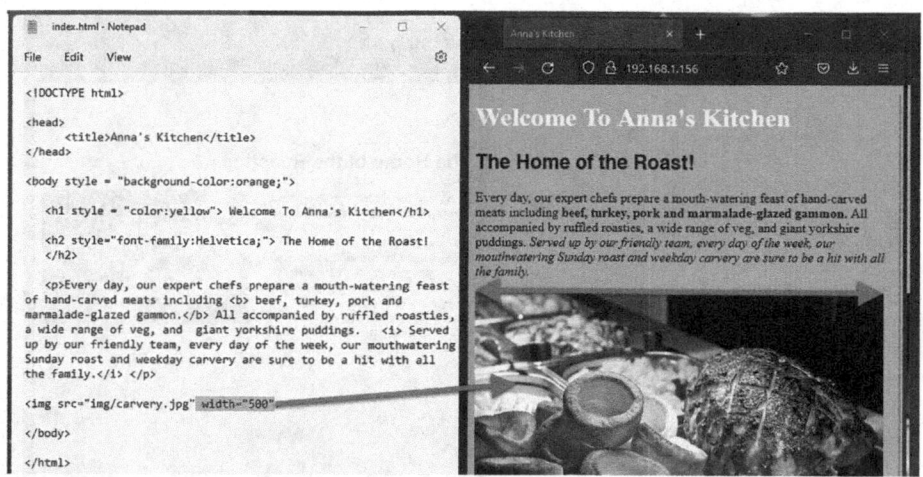

Figure 3-19. *Adjusting the Image Size*

Image Alignment

Images can be aligned to the left or to the right of the page just like text paragraphs using the alignment attribute.

In the preceding example, when we added the image to the web page, we just added it to the bottom of the page. The image is by default aligned to the left of the page.

You can align the images with your paragraphs on your page. This makes a much neater article to read.

To do this, you will need to nest the <img> element inside your paragraph <p> tag. This is simpler than it sounds.

I'm going to align the image to the right-hand side, using the align attribute, and put the <img> element after the paragraph's <p> tag. Have a look at the illustration in Figure 3-20.

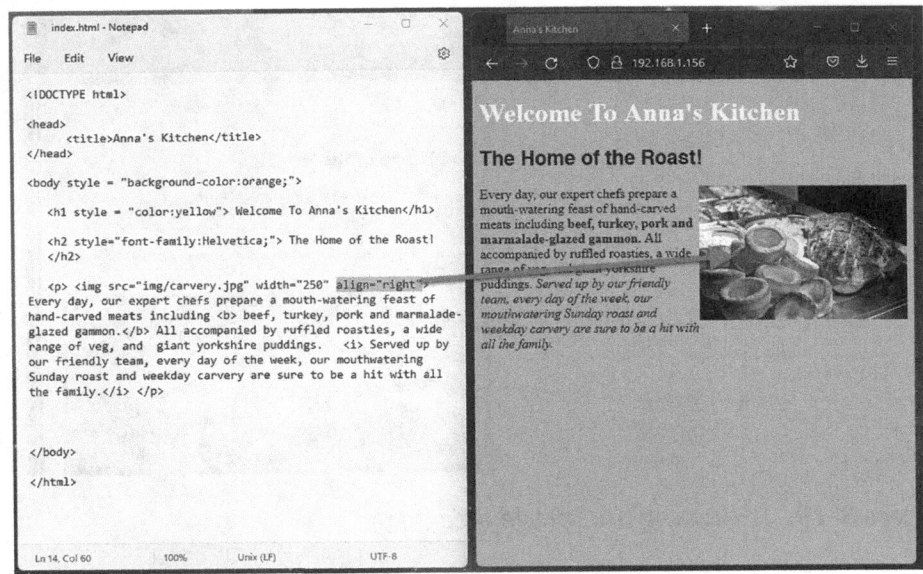

Figure 3-20. *Making the Image Fit*

Also, to make the image fit, you'll need to resize it using the width attribute on your <img> element. The width of our page is 540px, so roughly half that length would be sufficient. So set the width attribute to 250. Have a look at the highlighted line in the Notepad document earlier.

What happens if you change the align attribute to "left" or "middle"?

Background Image

You can add images to the background of many HTML elements such as the paragraph element or a table. For example, if I wanted to add a background image to the body of the document:

```
<body style = "background-image: url('img/img-bg.jpg')";
```

In Figure 3-21, I've highlighted where we've added the line.

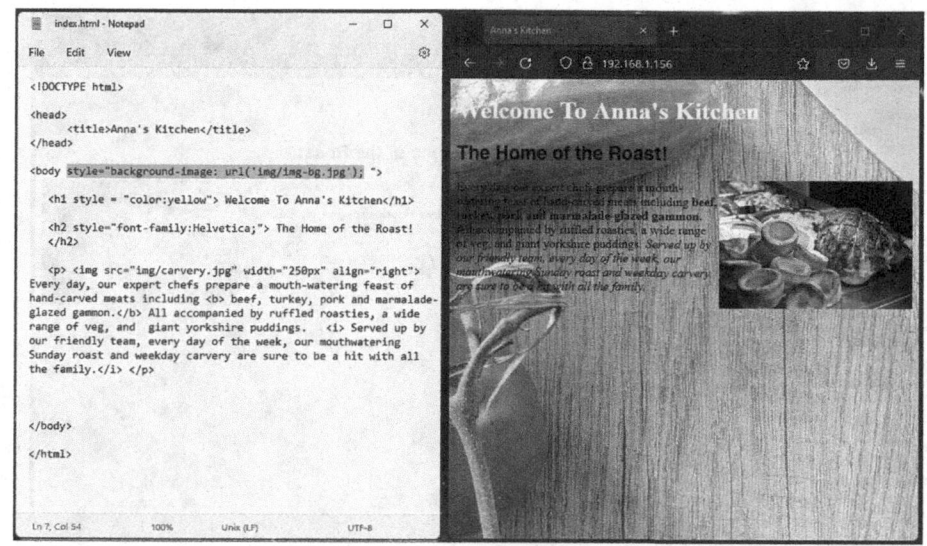

Figure 3-21. *Image Added to the Background*

Notice the image is too big for the screen.

We can resize the width using the background-size attribute. The first parameter is the width, and the second is the height:

```
background-size: width height
```

For example:

```
background-size: 100%;
```

You'll also notice that the background image is repeated down the page (Figure 3-22).

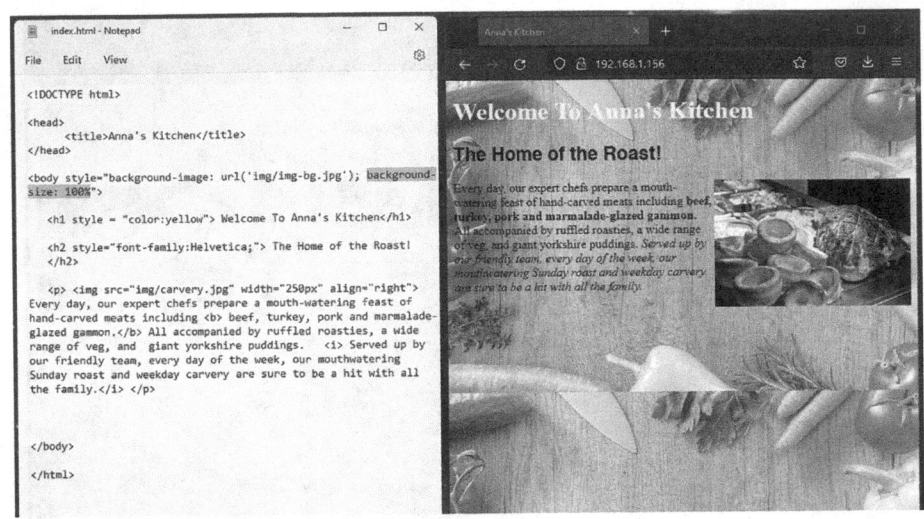

Figure 3-22. *Image Repeated in Background*

To change this, add

`background-repeat: no-repeat`

Let's take a look. Now you'll see the background only appears once (Figure 3-23).

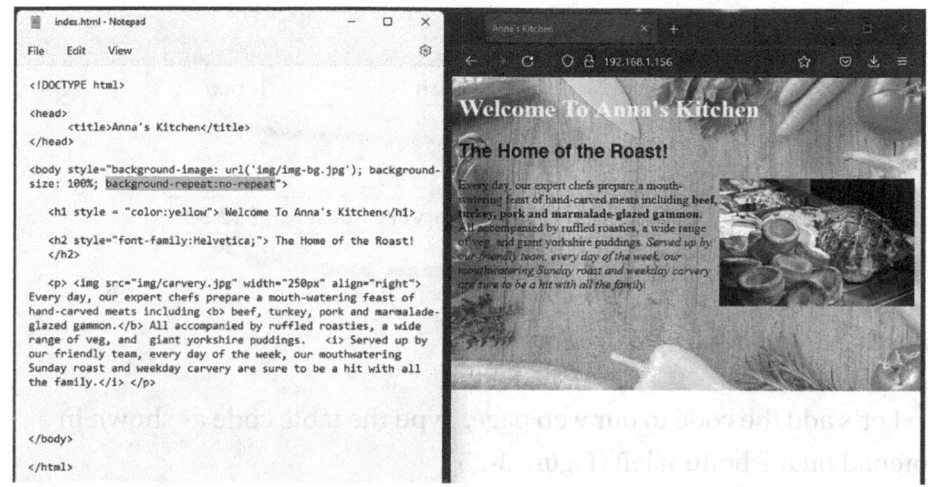

Figure 3-23. *Background Image Appears Once*

You can also add background images to other elements such as a paragraph:

```
<p style="background-image: url('img/img_bg.jpg');">
```

Adding Tables

To create a table, use the following tags:

```
<table> </table>
```

Inside these tags, you can use the following tags to define each table row:

```
<tr>...</tr>
```

Use the following tags to define each entry in that row – these become the columns:

```
<td>...</td>
```

Let's try an example (Figure 3-24).

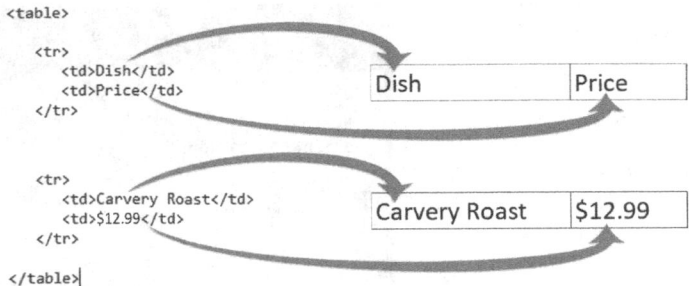

Figure 3-24. *Creating a Table*

Let's add the code to our web page. Type the table code as shown in Notepad on the bottom left (Figure 3-25).

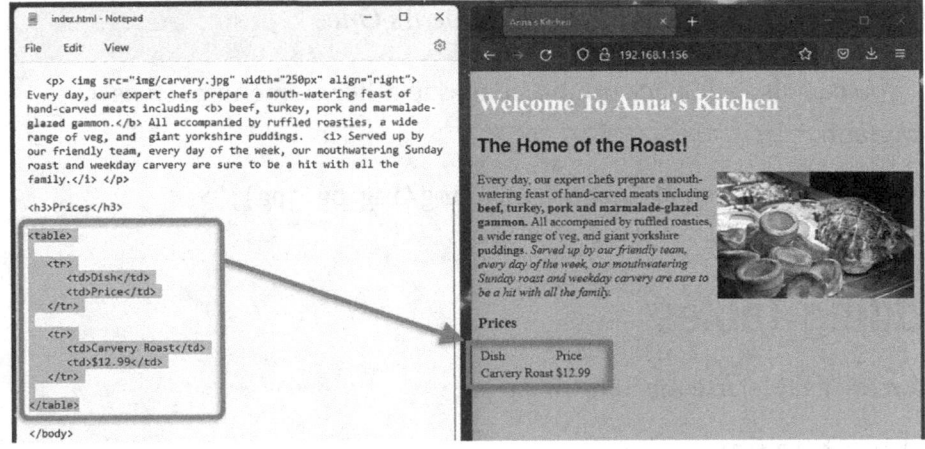

Figure 3-25. *Table on the Web Page*

Adding Links

Links can be added to your website using the anchor tags <a>...</a>. You can link to another website, another page, a document, or something to download.

Start with the anchor tag, then use the href attribute to specify the URL of the website or page you want to link to. Type the URL or page name between the speech marks:

```
<a href="menu.html">
```

Add the name of the link that will appear on the website between the tags:

```
View our Menu </a>
```

So, putting it all together, we get this:

```
<a href="menu.html"> View our Menu </a>
```

Try adding the line to the bottom of the document in Notepad. We've added the anchor tag between a paragraph tag to space out the lines (Figure 3-26).

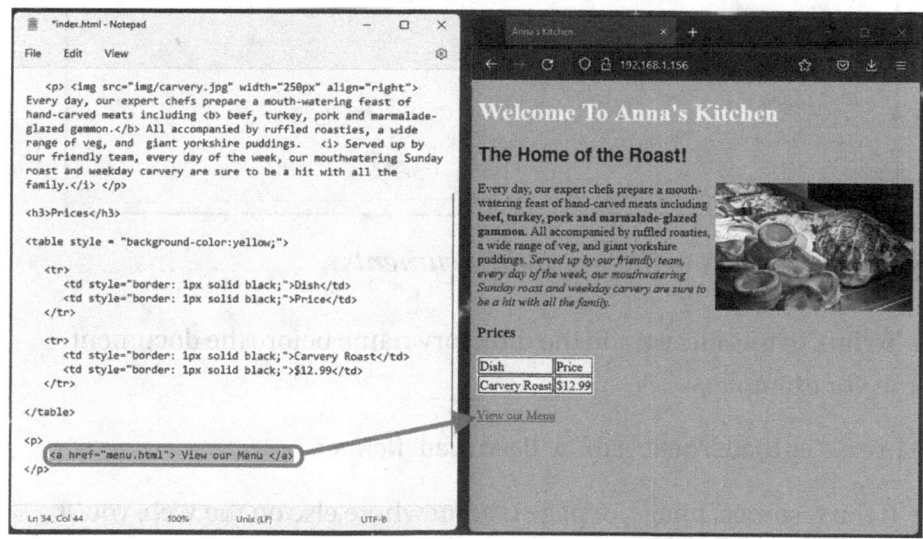

Figure 3-26. *Linking the Menu*

You can see the link in the web page on the right-hand side has blue underlined text. This indicates a link.

You can also link to specific files such as images, documents, or downloads.

For example, if you have a document in the folder called "uploads" in your PUBLIC_HTML or htdocs directory, you could have a PDF document in the "uploads" folder (Figure 3-27). On our personal web server, you can create a new folder in C:\Abyss Web Server\htdocs\ using the file explorer.

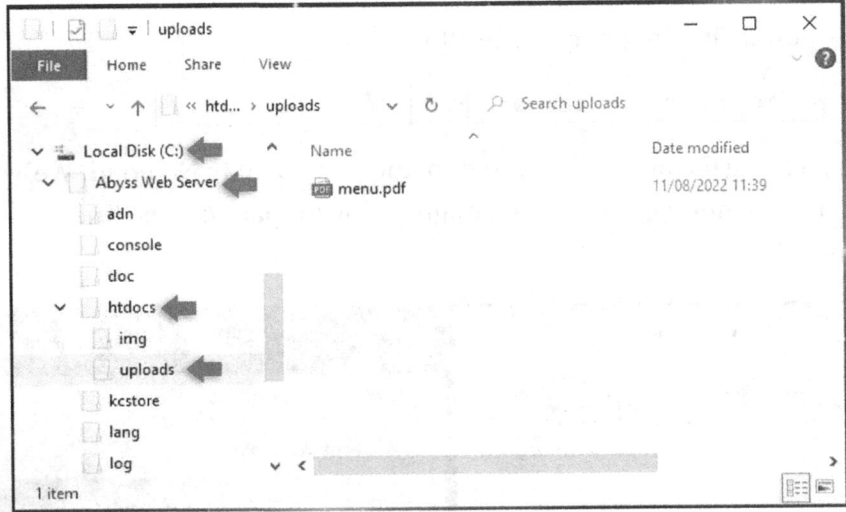

Figure 3-27. *Link to Images and Documents*

To link to this file, we add the directory name before the document name, for example:

```
<a href="uploads/menu.pdf"> Download Now </a>
```

If the resource, image, or page is somewhere else on the Web, you'll need to add the full address in the href attribute, for example:

```
www.ellumitechacademy.com/uploads/menu.pdf
```

or on our server:

```
localhost/uploads/menu.pdf
```

For 100% compatibility when linking to other sites and resources outside your own site, it is good practice to add the protocol to the beginning of your href URL, for example:

```
https://www.ellumitechacademy.com/uploads/menu.pdf
```

or on our server:

```
http://localhost/uploads/menu.pdf
```

Other protocols could be

```
ftp:
mailto:
file:
http:
https:
```

depending on where your resource is hosted.

Using Images As Links

You can also make an image into a link. To do this, all you need to do is insert your image:

```
<img src = "carvery.jpg">
```

between the anchor tags <a>...</a>. I want the image to link to the home page.

So you get something like this:

```
<a href = "menu.html"> <img src="carvery.jpg"> </a>
```

Let's take a look; add the code underneath. I have used an image called carvery.jpg in the images directory, so make sure you add

images/

before the file name in the src attribute of the <img> tag. Have a look at the code highlighted in the Notepad document on the left (Figure 3-28).

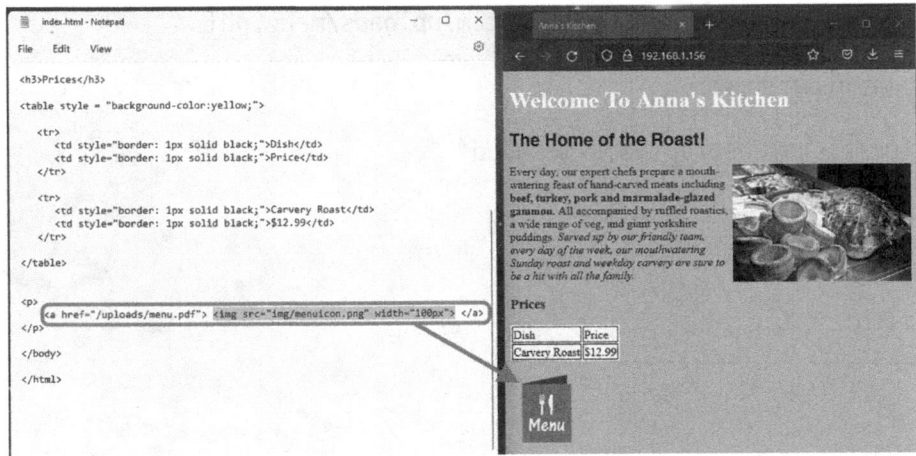

Figure 3-28. *Menu Link in the Image*

Notice the mouse pointer turns into a hand when you hover over the image (Figure 3-29). This indicates a link.

Figure 3-29. *The Menu Link Appears*

You can usually see the destination URL in the status bar at the bottom of your web browser.

Preserve Formatting

Sometimes, you might want your text to follow the exact format of how it is written in the HTML document. In these cases, you can use the preformatted tags:

`<pre>... </pre>`

Adding Lists

Unordered lists appear as bulleted lists. Ordered lists appear as numbered lists.

Unordered List

Use the <ul>...</ul> tags. For each item in the list, you will need to add text between the <li>...</li> tags (Figure 3-30).

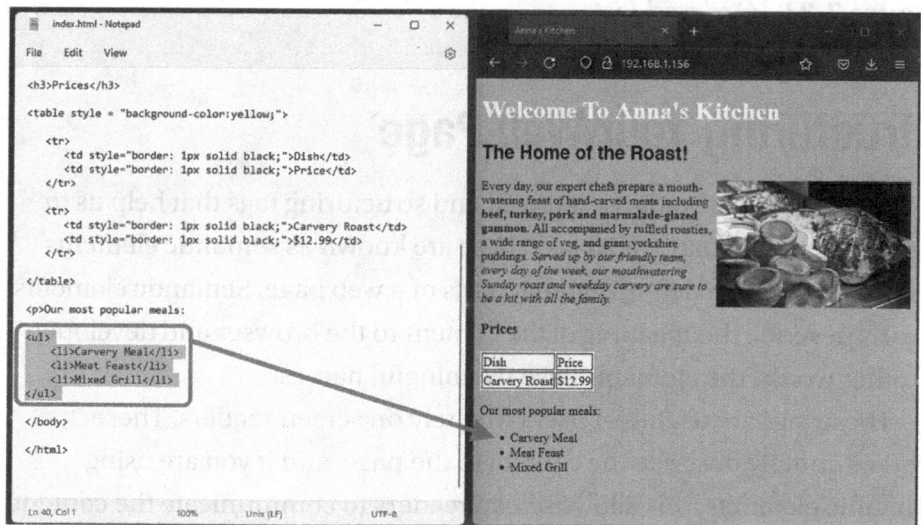

Figure 3-30. *Unordered List*

Ordered List

Use the <ol>...</ol> tags. For each item in the list, you will need to add the text between the <li>...</li> tags (Figure 3-31).

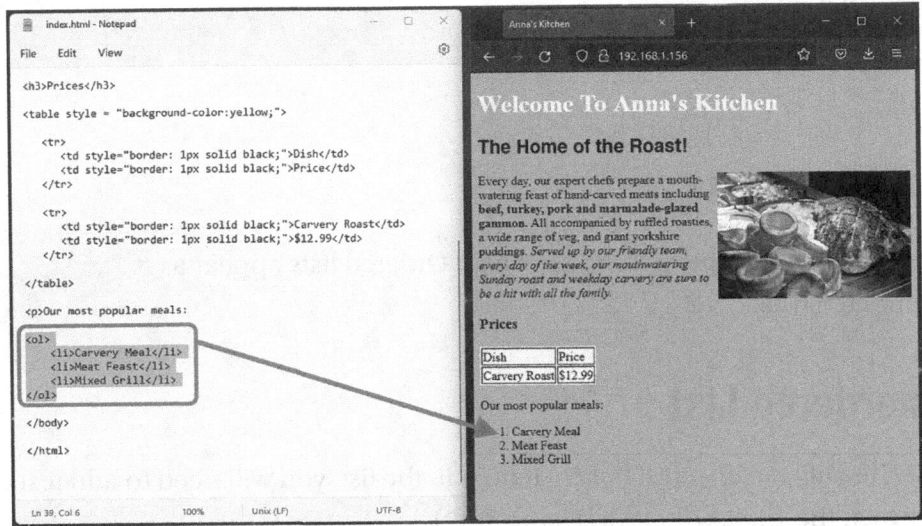

Figure 3-31. *Ordered List*

Structuring Your Web Page

HTML5 introduced some new layout and structuring tags that help us to define and format our web page. These are known as semantic elements and can be used to define different parts of a web page. Semantic elements clearly describe the meaning of the content to the browser and developer. In other words, the elements have meaningful names.

These tags are useful for users who rely on screen readers. These readers audibly describe the content of the page, and if you are using semantic elements, this allows screen readers to communicate the content of the page more accurately.

Search engines such as Google and Bing will use the semantic elements to identify and figure out which parts of your site contain the most important content.

Table 3-1 lists a few common elements.

Table 3-1. *Common Elements*

<header> ... </header>	A container for introductory content, page titles, or headings
<nav> ... </nav>	A section of a page used to contain navigation links such as site menus
<main> ... </main>	Contains the main content of the page
<section> ... </section>	A stand-alone section of the main page
<article> ... </article>	A self-contained section in a document or page that can be reused such as a blog article or widget
<aside> ... </aside>	Allows you to define some content aside from the main content such as a sidebar
<footer> ... </footer>	Contains information such as footnotes, author, and copyright data
<figure> ... </figure>	Contains photos, images, illustrations, or diagrams
<figcaption> ... </figcaption>	Allows you to define a caption for a <figure> element
<summary> ... </summary>	Allows you to define a visible heading for the <details> element
<details> ... </details>	Allows you to specify content that the user can open and close
<div class=" "> ... </div>	Defines a division or a section in an HTML document and can be used as a container for HTML elements styled with CSS or manipulated using the class or id attribute. See Chapter 4

Let's start adding these to the relevant sections of our HTML page. Our page has a header "Welcome to Anna's Kitchen," so we can surround that with the <header> tags, and a navigation bar, so we can surround the nav image map with the <nav> tags (Figure 3-32).

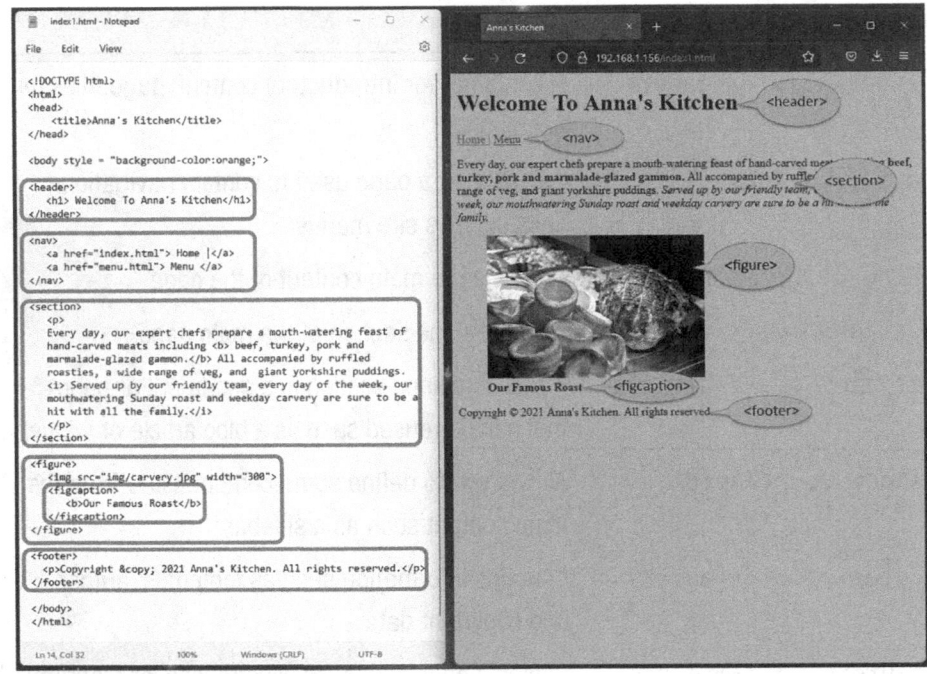

Figure 3-32. *Tags*

The main content can go in a <section> tag, any images can go in the <figure> tab, and we can add a footer using the <footer> tags.

Lab Exercises

1. Open a new text file and save it as ch03.html.

2. Write the basic structure of an HTML document.

3. How do you write bold text using HTML elements?

4. How to define the document's body?

5. How do you create headings using HTML elements?

6. In the HTML document ch03.html, create a heading.

7. Change the background color to #E2E0E2 or one of your own choice.

8. Start a new paragraph, then add a paragraph of text.

9. Insert a hyperlink to the document you created in the previous chapter (ch02.html).

Summary

- When using the local Abyss Server on your computer, save documents to **C:\Abyss Web Server\htdocs**.

- To access the website on your computer with a browser, use **http://127.0.0.1**.

- Main heading style: **<h1>...</h1>**

- Subheading style: **<h2>...</h2>**

- Minor heading style: **<h3>...</h3>**

- Bold text: **<b>...</b>**

- Italic text: **<i>...</i>**

- Paragraph text: **<p>...</p>**

- Add a style attribute to change color, for example, **<H1 style = "color:Yellow;">**.

- Add a style attribute to change font, for example, **<H1 style = "font-family:Helvetica;">**.

- To add a table, use **\<table\> \</table\>**.

- To define each table row, use **\<tr\>...\</tr\>**.

- To define data to that row, use **\<td\>...\</td\>**.

- Use the img element to add an image: **\<img src = " "
width = " "\>**.

- Use the anchor element to define hyperlinks:
\<a href = " "\>.

CHAPTER 4

Cascading Style Sheets

Cascading Style Sheets (CSS) are used to define and customize the styles and layouts for your web pages. This means you can create style sheets to alter the design, layout, and responsiveness to different screen sizes on various devices from computers to smartphones.

CSS describes how HTML elements are to be displayed on screen and controls the layout of multiple web pages all at once. This is because the style sheets are stored in separate CSS files and are linked to the HTML document.

CSS solved a big problem. HTML was never originally intended to contain tags for formatting a web page and was created to describe the content of said web page. When more formatting attributes were added to the HTML 3.2 specification, it became a total nightmare for web developers to design and maintain websites. This is because fonts, formatting, layout, and color information were added to every single HTML tag on every page, so making changes and maintaining a website was a long and expensive process.

To solve this problem, the World Wide Web Consortium (W3C) created and introduced CSS. CSS removed the style formatting from the HTML page and allowed the developer to include the formatting and layout information in a separate file which could be included in all the other HTML pages that make up the website.

© Kevin Wilson 2023
K. Wilson, *The Absolute Beginner's Guide to HTML and CSS*,
https://doi.org/10.1007/978-1-4842-9250-1_4

The word "cascading" means that styling rules flow down from several sources. This means that CSS has a hierarchy, and styles of a higher precedence will overwrite styles of a lower precedence. In other words, styles lower down the hierarchy have higher priority over those higher up.

There are three methods you can use to include CSS styles in your HTML document.

First, you can include them inline using the style attribute within the opening tag:

```
<h1 style="color:blue; font-size:14px;"> Heading 1</h1>
```

You can embed the styles using the <style> element in the head section of a document:

```
<head>
    <style>
        H1 {
            color:blue;
            font-size:14px;"
        }
    </style>
</head>
```

You can include CSS styles saved in another file using the <link> element with the href attribute pointing to the CSS file:

```
<link rel="stylesheet" href="style.css">
```

External CSS Files

It is recommended that you add your CSS declarations to a separate text file and link that file into all the relevant HTML files (Figure 4-1). In this way, you have all your style declarations in one place and can change things easily.

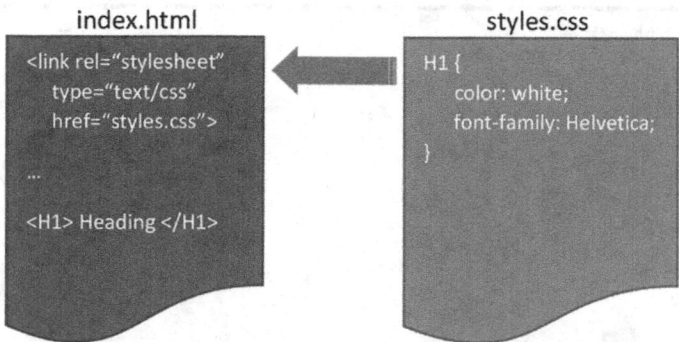

Figure 4-1. *Linking a CSS File into an HTML Page*

As we have seen in the previous chapter, we had to style each element every time we use it. These are known as inline styles and are very inefficient. What happens if we have a large website and we've styled every heading to be 20px, white, using the Helvetica font, and the client wants to change the color of the text or the font. We'd have to go through every instance and change it. Sounds like a nightmare to me.

A much better way is to define all the elements, tags, and so on using a style sheet. This is where CSS shows its true power. If the client came with the preceding request, and we used CSS style sheets, we would only have to change the declaration in the CSS, and every instance would change throughout the whole site.

Create a text file with the .CSS file extension and make sure it's in the same directory as your HTML files (Figure 4-2).

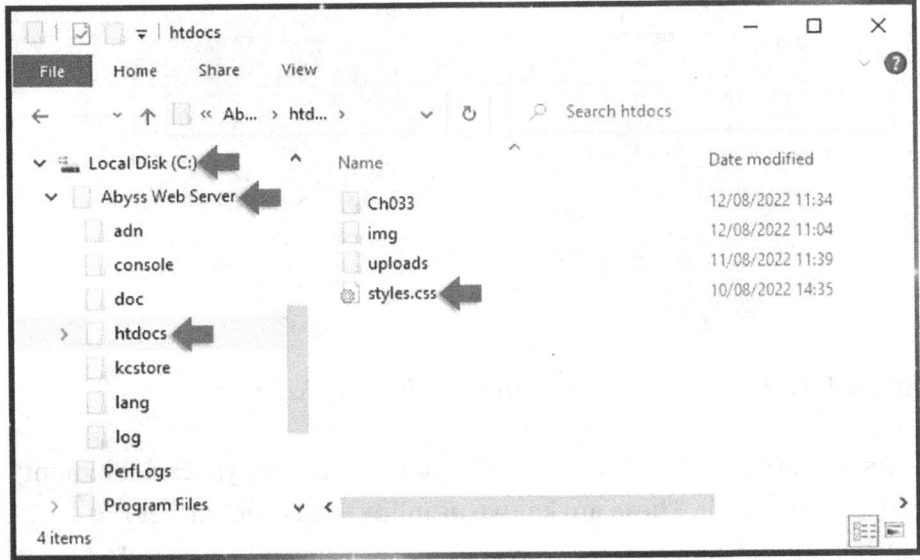

Figure 4-2. *.CSS Text File*

Add this line in the <head> section of each HTML file that is to be styled using the declarations contained in the CSS file. Use the href attribute to point to the CSS file:

```
<link rel="stylesheet" type="text/css" href="styles.css">
```

CSS Syntax

Let's take a look at the basic syntax of a CSS rule. As you can see in Figure 4-3, the CSS rule consists of a selector and a declaration block.

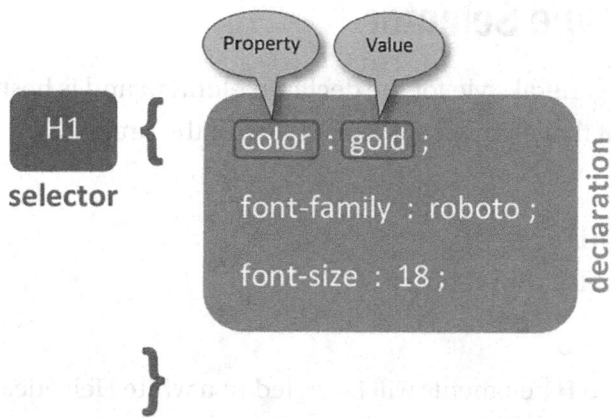

Figure 4-3. *CSS Syntax*

The selector points to the HTML or element you want to style. The declaration block starts with a curly brace and contains one or more style declarations separated by semicolons. Each declaration includes a CSS property name and a value, separated by a colon.

You can use these to configure the styles of the classes and selectors using various properties as you can see in Figure 4-4.

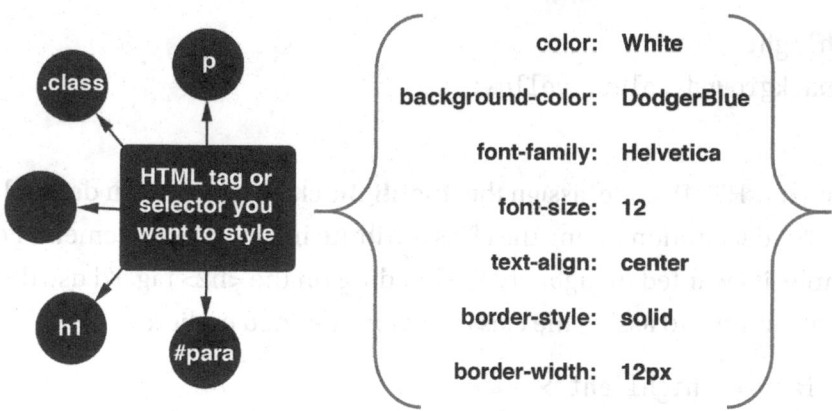

Figure 4-4. *Styling Various CSS Selectors*

Element Type Selector

This creates a general style for the declared element and is best used when all instances of that element are to be styled in the same way:

```
H1 {
    color: white;
    font-family: Helvetica;
}
```

Here, all the H1 elements will be styled in a white Helvetica font.

Class Selector

A class selector is used to apply styles to a specific HTML element. You can name the class anything you want, and it must begin with a dot (or period). Use class selectors when you want to style multiple elements throughout the page or site with the same look or layout.

So in this example, I'm creating a highlight style I can apply to various HTML elements such as headings <H1> and <H2> or a paragraph <p>:

```
.highlight {
    background-color: yellow;
}
```

In your HTML code, assign the **.highlight** class selector you defined in your CSS declarations using the class attribute in any HTML element. For example, if I wanted to highlight the heading on the <h2> tag, I'd use the class attribute and assign the class selector I defined earlier:

```
<h2 class = "highlight">
    The Home of the Roast
</h2>
```

Similarly, if I wanted to highlight the paragraph

```
<p class = "highlight">
    Every day, our expert chefs...
</p>
```

Let's add this to our little web page. I've declared the **.highlight** class in the styles.css file. You can see it highlighted in Figure 4-5. I've applied the **.highlight** class selector to the <h2> HTML tag highlighted in the index. html file.

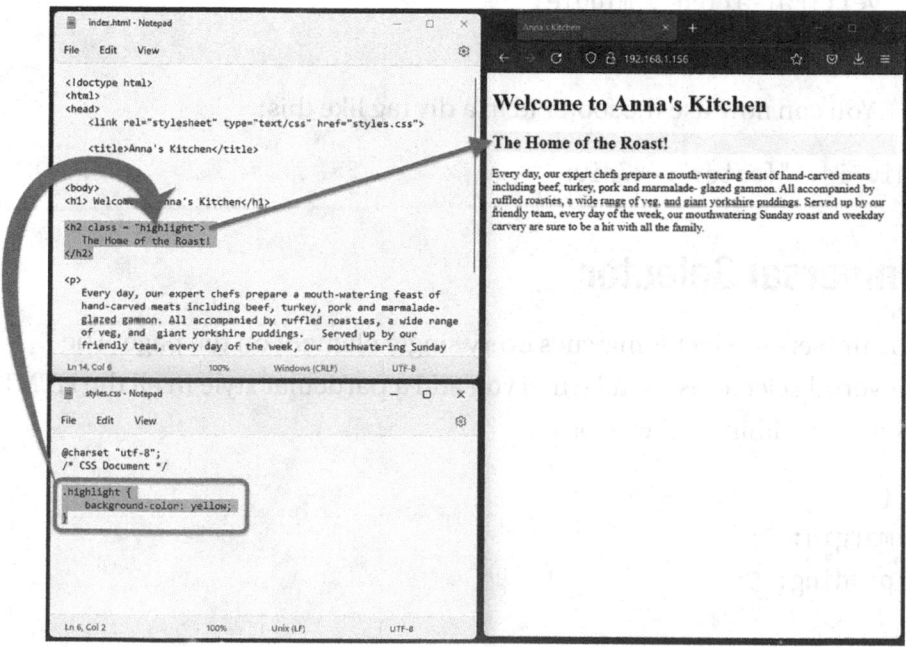

Figure 4-5. *.highlight Class*

ID Selector

The ID selector targets a single element and can only be used once per page.

ID selectors are defined in the CSS declarations using a hashtag # and should only be used when you have a single element on the page that will have that particular style or layout.

Here, we're going to set the background color of the footer to gold, and we want the footer to be 100 pixels high, the text aligned in the center, and the text aligned in the middle vertically:

```
#footer {
    background-color : gold;
    line-height : 50px;
    text-align : center;
    vertical-align : middle;
}
```

You can now use the footer id in a div tag like this:

```
<div id= "footer"> </div>
```

Universal Selector

The universal selector matches every single element on the page. The universal selector is useful when you add a particular style in all the HTML elements within your web page:

```
* {
  margin: 5;
  padding: 5;
}
```

Grouping Selectors

If you want to style more than one selector with the same styles, you can do this by grouping the selectors together.

For example, if I wanted to create a style where all my headings are in the center and are colored gold, instead of declaring them all individually as we see as follows:

```
h1 {
    text-align: center;
    color: gold;
}

h2 {
    text-align: center;
    color: gold;
}

h3 {
    text-align: center;
    color: gold;
}
```

I can group all the selectors together followed by the declarations:

```
h1, h2, h3 {
    text-align: center;
    color: gold;
}
```

This is much more efficient and allows you to declare the styles once.

Styling Text

If I wanted to style the H1 tag for my headings, I could write something like this in the styles.css file:

```
H1 {
    font-color: yellow;
    font-family: Roboto;
}
```

This would style all the H1 tags used subsequently in the HTML file.

If I wanted to style my subheadings <H2>, I can do the same. I want to change the font color to yellow with a Roboto font, but this time I want to make the text heavier or more bold. I can do this by adding the font-weight property:

```
H2 {
    color: yellow;
    font-family: Roboto;
    font-weight: 400;
}
```

Let's take a look at what happens when we add the code to our website (Figure 4-6).

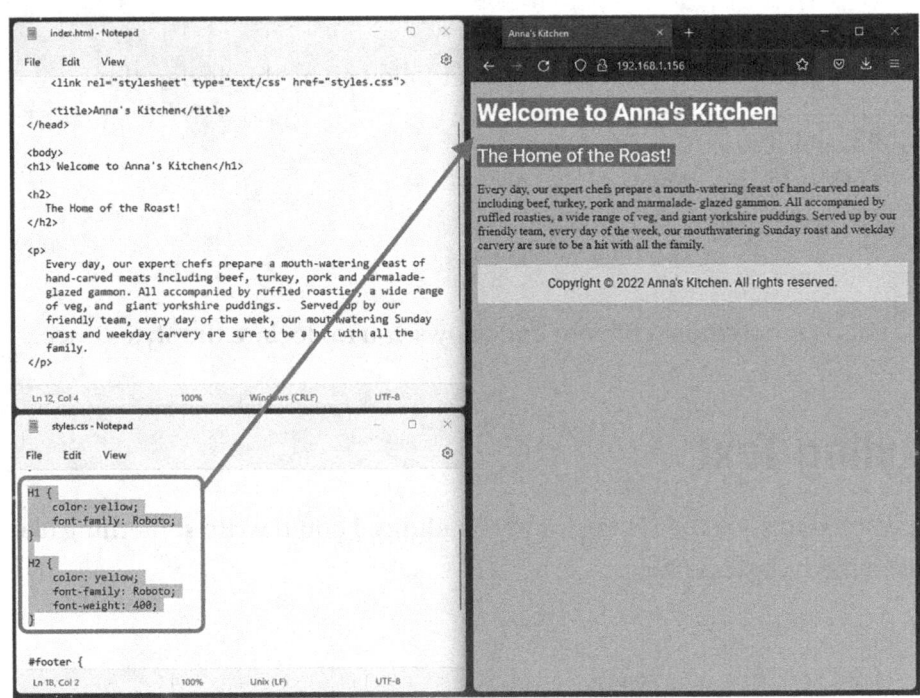

Figure 4-6. *Adding Color to the Website*

As you can see in Figure 4-7, the titles have changed font and color.

Welcome to Anna's Kitchen

The Home of the Roast!

Every day, our expert chefs prepare a mouth-watering feast of hand-carved meats including beef, turkey, pork and marmalade- glazed gammon. All accompanied by ruffled roasties, a wide range of veg, and giant yorkshire puddings. Served up by our friendly team, every day of the week, our mouthwatering Sunday roast and weekday carvery are sure to be a hit with all the family.

Copyright © 2022 Anna's Kitchen. All rights reserved.

Welcome to Anna's Kitchen

The Home of the Roast!

Every day, our expert chefs prepare a mouth-watering feast of hand-carved meats including beef, turkey, pork and marmalade- glazed gammon. All accompanied by ruffled roasties, a wide range of veg, and giant yorkshire puddings. Served up by our friendly team, every day of the week, our mouthwatering Sunday roast and weekday carvery are sure to be a hit with all the family.

Copyright © 2022 Anna's Kitchen. All rights reserved.

Figure 4-7. *Changing Font Color*

Try changing the font color and alignment in the styles.css file and see what happens.

Specifying Colors

You can specify colors using the following formats:

- A Color keyword such as "red," "green," "blue," "transparent," "orange," etc.

- A hex value such as "#000000", "#00A500", "#FFFFFF", etc.

- An RGB value such as "rgb(255, 255, 0)"

Keyword

You can use a keyword for the color you want such as black, white, navy, silver, yellow, orange, darkorange, gold, and so on. See Appendix C for the full list. For example:

```
h1 {
    color: orange;
}
```

Hex Value

A hex value represents colors using a six-digit code preceded by a hash character. The code is split into three two-digit hex numbers that represent the amount of red, green, and blue in varying intensities to create the color you want. The values are represented using the hexadecimal numbering scheme, not decimal. See Appendix C for the full list.

Hex	0	1	2	3	4	5	6	7	8	9	A	B	C	D	E	F
Decimal	0	1	2	3	4	5	6	7	8	9	10	11	12	13	14	15

So, for example, to create orange, we need full red, a bit of green, and no blue. FF in hex is 255 in decimal; A5 in hex is 165 in decimal. The hex code would be

Red	Green	Blue
FF	A5	00

We can use this hex code to represent the color we want:

```
h1 {
    color: #FFA500;
}
```

RGB Value

You can specify a color using the rgb() function. This function accepts three values from 0 to 255, which specify the amount of red, green, and blue in varying intensities to create the color you want. So, to create orange, we need red mixed with a little bit of green but no blue.

Red	Green	Blue
255	165	0

```
h1 {
    color: rgb(255, 165, 0);
}
```

See Appendix C for the full list of color codes.

Understanding Measurement Units

To control the size of certain objects such as fonts or images, the sizes are specified using various units. There are two types: absolute and relative.

Units that are absolute are the same size regardless of the parent element or window size. Table 4-1 shows some examples.

Table 4-1. *Unit Meaning*

Unit	Meaning
in	Inch
mm	Millimeter
px	Short for pixels and is usually used to measure the dimensions of an image
pt	Short for points and is used to measure the size of a font

Units that are relative scale in relation to the parent element or window size depending on the unit used. Here are some examples:

Unit	Meaning
em	Relative to the current font size of the element. If a font is 12pt, each em unit would be 12pt, so 2em would be 12 x 2 which is 24pt, similarly 1.5em would be 18pt
%	Relative to the parent element or window size

Padding, Margins, and Borders

HTML elements can be considered as boxes. The CSS box model is essentially a box that wraps around every HTML element. Around the content are various layers; the first is padding, then the border, then the margin (Figure 4-8).

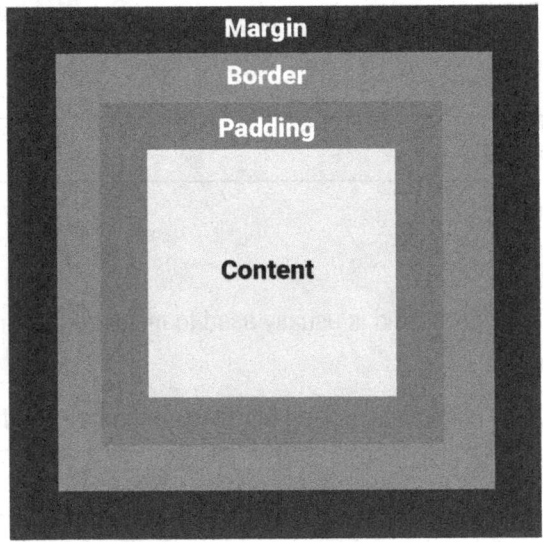

Figure 4-8. *The Box Model*

Let's take a look at the different parts. In Figure 4-8, we can see that

- The content of the box is where text and images appear.

- The padding property is used to add space around the content, inside of the defined border.

- The margin property is used to add space around the content, outside of the defined border.

- The border-style property specifies what kind of border to display.

So, for example, let's add a style to our H1 heading:

```
.myClass {
  padding: 10px;
  border: solid 5px black;
  margin: 20px;
}
```

When we open the HTML page in the web browser, we will see something like Figure 4-9.

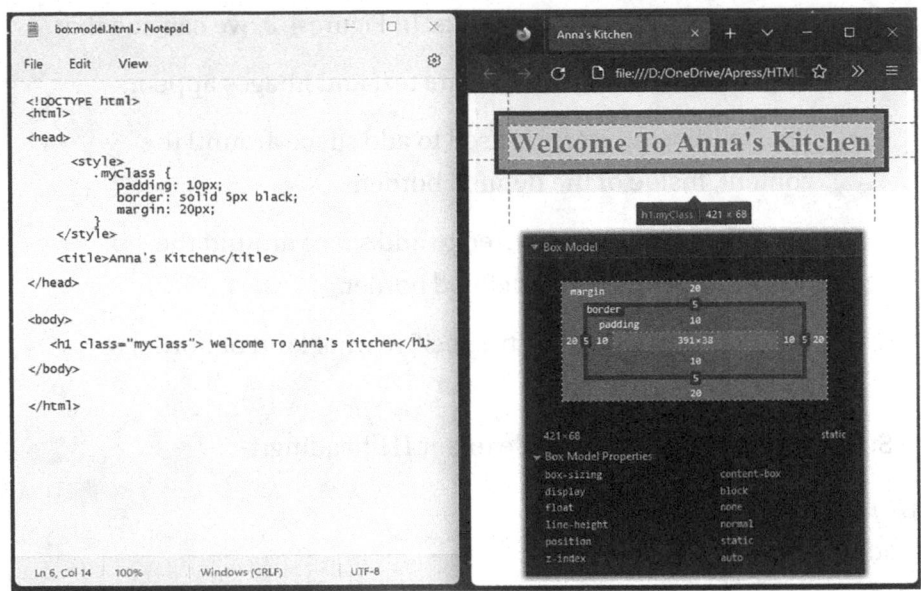

Figure 4-9. *Boxes in Use*

If you look in the web browser, you can see the box model around the heading. The dotted lines mark the edge of the content. Then we see 10px of padding, then a 5px thick black border, and 20px margin outside the border.

Layouts

In the previous section, the website we've been working on is very linear, meaning each section is just listed under the next. With style sheets, you're not just limited to restyling HTML tags, you can define layouts and sections.

Flexbox

Flexbox is a layout module designed for laying out content in one dimension (row or column, not both at the same time) and works best with items that have different sizes. Flexbox consists of **flex containers** (called the parent elements) that contain **flex items** (called the child elements) (Figure 4-10).

Figure 4-10. *Flexbox Container*

The items in the flex container can be laid out in any direction and can "flex" their sizes which means the items can grow to fill unused space or shrink depending on the screen size.

We can create a container in our CSS code like this:

```
.flex-container {
  display: flex;
}
```

The flex property in the display element sets how a flex item will grow or shrink to fit the space available in its container.

We can change the container direction to span rows or columns (Figure 4-11).

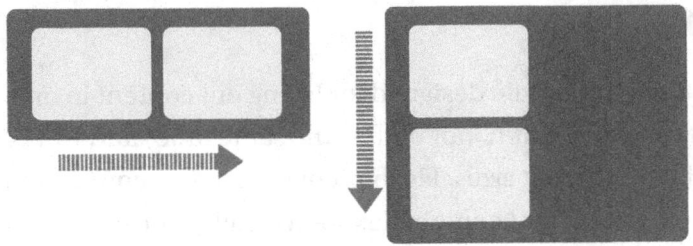

Figure 4-11. *Flexbox Container Spanning Rows and Columns*

If we want the items to be stacked side by side in rows (Figure 4-12). This is the default.

Figure 4-12. *Flexbox Container Spanning Rows*

To do this, we use **flex-direction: rows**:

```
.flex-container {
  display: flex;
  flex-direction: row;
}
```

If we want the items to be stacked on top of each other in columns (Figure 4-13),

Figure 4-13. *Flexbox Container Spanning Columns*

To do this, use **flex-direction: columns**:

```
.flex-container {
  display: flex;
  flex-direction: column;
}
```

We can specify whether we want the items to wrap or not. Here, the items will wrap to the next row if the screen size is smaller (Figure 4-14).

Figure 4-14. *Flexbox Container Wrapping*

In this example, we're going to wrap the contents, so we add **flex-wrap: wrap**:

```
.flex-container {
  display: flex;
  flex-direction: row;
  flex-wrap: wrap;
}
```

Now that we have created the container, we can add some items using the <div> element. In our HTML code, we can add

```
<div class="flex-container">
  <div> This is content inside item </div>
  <div> <img src="img/bluebox.png"> </div>
  <div> <img src="img/bluebox.png"> </div>
</div>
```

The order property specifies the order of the flex items:

```
<div class="flex-container">
  <div style="order: 3"> This is content inside item </div>
  <div style="order: 1"> <img src="img/bluebox.png"> </div>
  <div style="order: 2"> <img src="img/bluebox.png"> </div>

</div>
```

If we want to style the items inside the container, we can use the greater than ">" symbol:

```
.flex-container-name > child-item-name {

...

}
```

This symbol is used to select the element with a specific parent. Since each item in the flex-container is specified with a <div> element, these are the child items. So the child-item-name we want is div, and it belongs to flex-container. Now let's change the background color to light gray, then add a margin and some padding to space out the items:

```
.flex-container > div {
  background-color: #f1f1f1;
  margin: 10px;
  padding: 10px;
}
```

In Figure 4-15, we have our HTML code open on the top left, with our CSS code open on the bottom left. On the right, we can see what it looks like in a web browser. What happens when you resize the width of the browser window (Figure 4-15)?

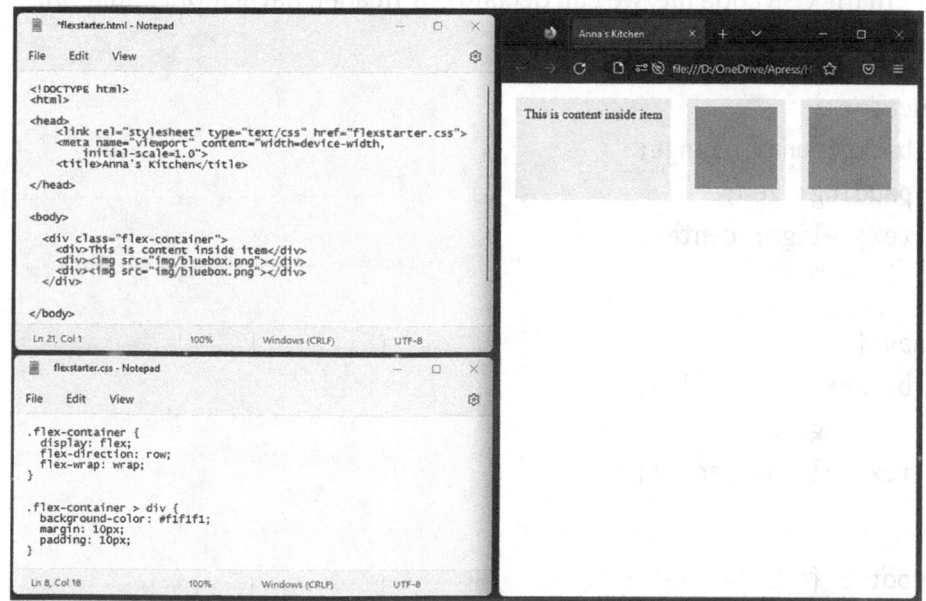

Figure 4-15. *Resizing*

95

Putting Flexbox into Practice

Let's create a layout for our website (Figure 4-16). Here, we want to create a header and a navigation bar along the top of the page; then underneath, we want to create the site content with a sidebar to the right – this is the only part we're using flexbox. Finally, we want to add a footer to the page.

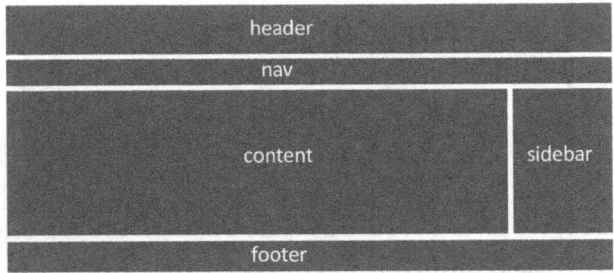

Figure 4-16. *Website Layout*

In the CSS code file, we can declare our header, navigation, and footer using simple CSS class selectors:

```
.header {
  background: orange;
  padding: 2em;
  text-align: center;
}

.nav {
  background: yellow;
  padding: 1em;
  text-align: center;
}

.footer {
  background: orange;
  padding: 1em;
}
```

When we get to the content and sidebar, this is where we want to use flexbox. We can create our container:

```
.flex-container {
  display: flex;
  flex-direction: row;
}
```

Then create the content and sidebar as child items of the container. Add some padding to space out the content, and set the background color of the sidebar to gray:

```
.flex-container > .content {
  padding: 10px;

}
```

```
.flex-container > .sidebar {
  background-color: #f1f1f1;
  padding: 10px;

}
```

Now in our HTML code file, we can add our header and nav bar using the <div> element. Just add the name of the selector defining the header using the "class" attribute in the opening <div> tag. Add the content to display between the opening and closing <div> tags:

```
<div class="header">
    <h1> Welcome To Anna's Kitchen</h1>
    <b> The Home of the Roast! </b>
</div>
```

Do the same for the nav bar:

```
<div class="nav">
    <a href="index.html"> Home </a> |
    <a href="menu.html"> Menu </a> |
    <a href="book.html"> Book a Table </a>
</div>
```

Next, we need to create our flexbox container to contain the content and sidebar. We can add the flex-container using the "class" attribute in the opening <div> tag:

```
<div class="flex-container">
```

Then inside the flex-container <div> element we declared earlier, we can add another <div> element with the content child item using the "class" attribute in the opening <div> tag:

```
<div class="content">
    <p>
    Every day, our expert chefs prepare a mouth-watering
    feast of
    hand-carved meats including <b> beef, turkey, pork and
    marmalade-
    glazed gammon.</b> All accompanied by ruffled
    roasties, a wide
    range of veg, and  giant yorkshire puddings.   <i> Served
    up by our
    friendly team, every day of the week, our
    mouthwatering Sunday
    roast and weekday carvery are sure to be a hit
    with all the
    family.</i> </p>
</div>
```

And do the same with the sidebar:

<div class="sidebar">

```
  <img src="img/menumap.png" width="220px"
  usemap="#foodmenu">
  <map name = "foodmenu">
    <area shape= "rect" coords = "0,0,220,202" href =
    "menu1.htm">
    <area shape= "rect" coords = "0,202,220,395" href =
    "menu2.htm">
    <area shape= "rect" coords = "0,395,220,596" href =
    "menu3.htm">
  </map>
</div>
```

Remember to close the **flex-container** with

```
</div>
```

We will see something like Figure 4-17.

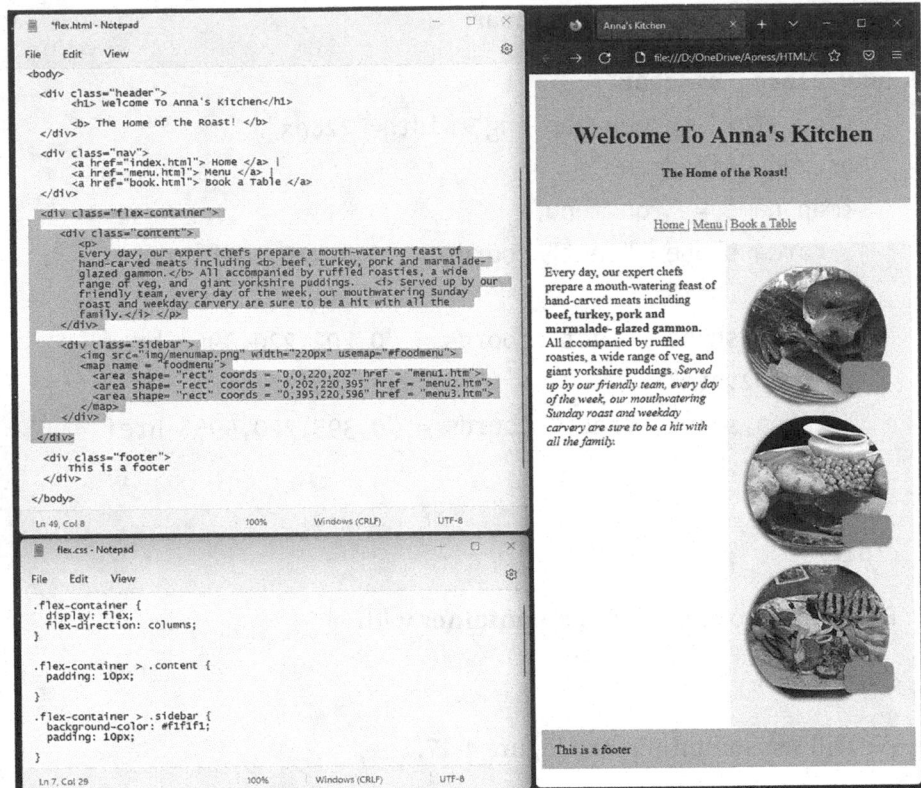

Figure 4-17. *Flex Container*

Notice that things don't wrap when we resize the window. To make things wrap, we need to add the flex attribute to the container:

```
.flex-container {
  display: flex;
  flex-direction: row;
  flex-wrap: wrap;
}
```

as well as to the children:

```
flex: flex-grow flex-shrink flex-basis;
```

100

flex-grow specifies how much the item will grow relative to the rest of the flexible items by a factor. **flex-grow: 0** means items won't grow. **flex-grow: 1** means items can grow larger than their flex-basis.

flex-shrink specifies how much the item will shrink relative to the rest of the flexible items. **flex-shrink: 1** means items can shrink smaller than their flex-basis.

flex-basis is the length of the item measured in "%", "px", or "em". You can also have values: "auto" or "inherit."

For example, if I add the following to the content item:

```
flex: 1 1 250px;
```

what does this mean?

flex-grow: 1 means items can grow larger than their flex-basis.

flex-shrink: 1 means items can shrink smaller than their flex-basis.

flex: 250px means once the first row gets to a point where there is not enough space to place another 250px item, a new flex line is created for the items. As the items can grow, they will expand larger than 250px in order to fill each row completely. If there is only one item on the final line, it will stretch to fill the entire line.

So we end up with this:

```
.flex-container > .content {
  flex: 1 1 250px;
  padding: 10px;

}

.flex-container > .sidebar {
  flex: 1 1 50px;
  background-color: #f1f1f1;
  padding: 10px;

}
```

Let's take a look at what this looks like in a browser (Figure 4-18).

101

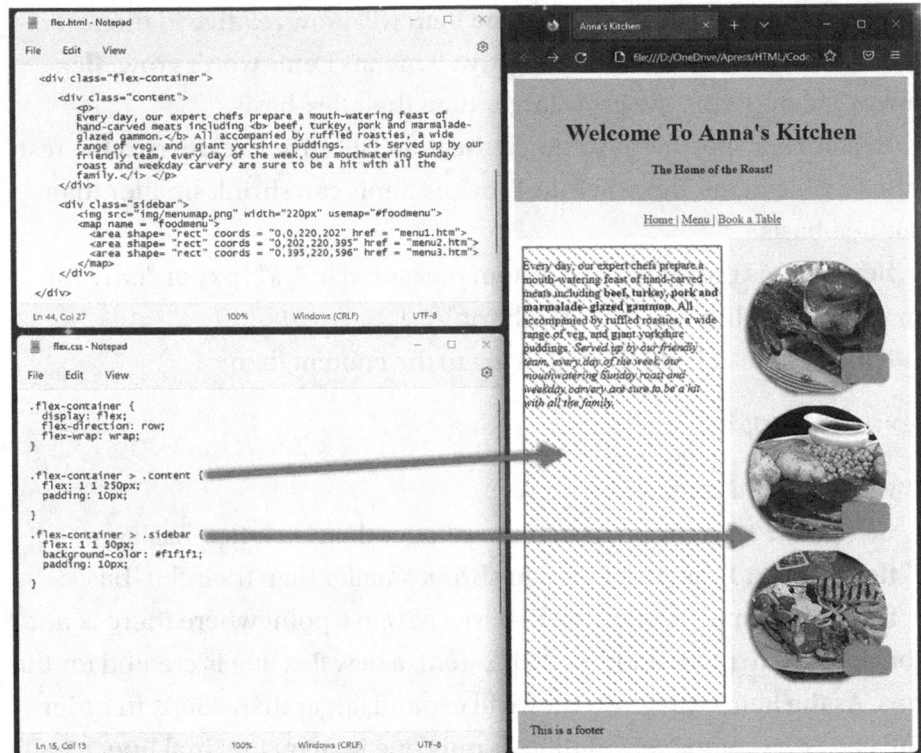

Figure 4-18. *Flex Containers in the Browser*

What happens when you resize the browser window? Notice how they stretch when we extend the width of the browser. Also, notice how the sidebar wraps when we reduce the width of the browser. It will wrap when the content gets to 250px (Figure 4-19).

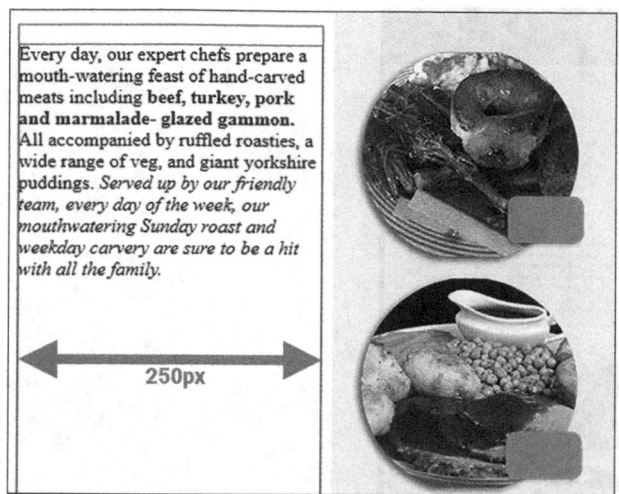

Figure 4-19. *The Sidebar Sized at 250px*

Let's try it. Here, we've reduced the browser width and expanded the width to see what happens (Figure 4-20).

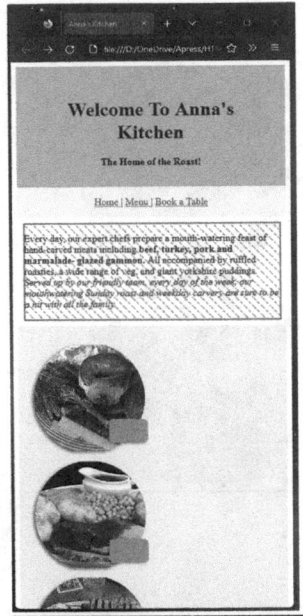
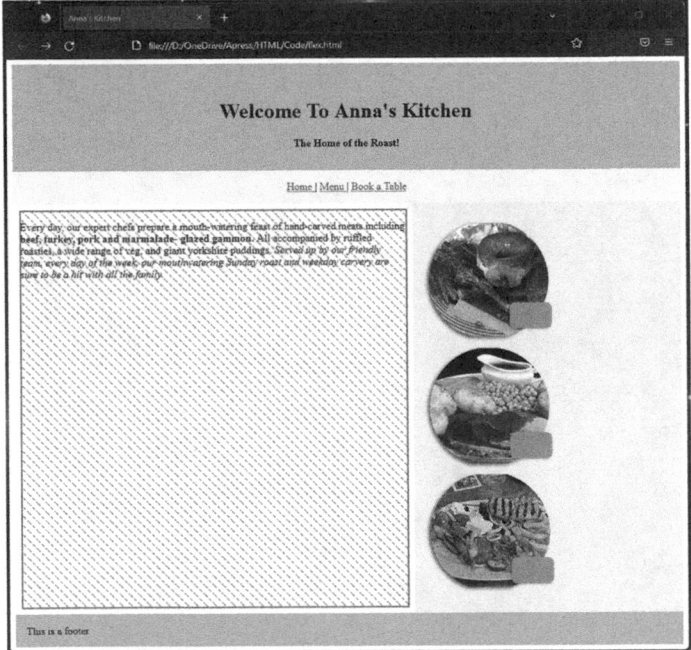

Figure 4-20. *The Width Reduced and Expanded*

Keep in mind that flexbox can only handle rows or columns, not both.

CSS Grid

A CSS grid layout is a two-dimensional grid-based layout system with rows and columns that is designed to make it easier to lay out web pages and enables a developer to align elements into columns and rows. A CSS grid is a perfect candidate for whole page layouts.

In Figure 4-21, the vertical lines are called columns, and the horizontal lines are called rows. The spaces between each column/row are called row gaps. Grid items such as images or text can be aligned along the rows and columns of the grid and are called grid items (Figure 4-22).

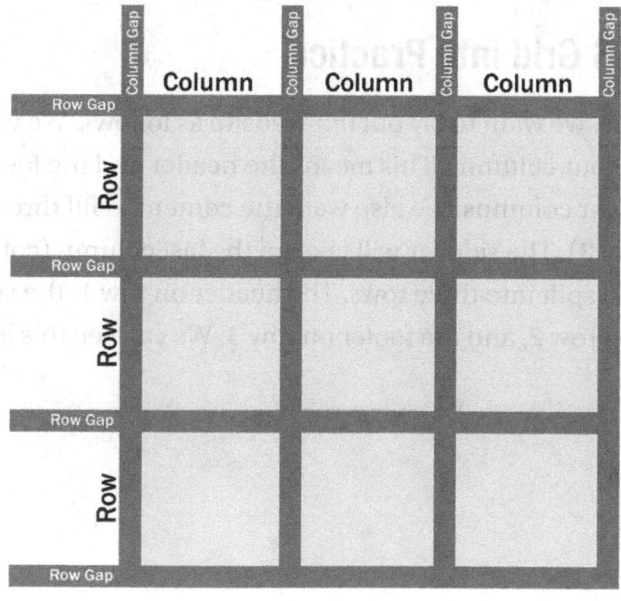

Figure 4-21. *CSS Grid*

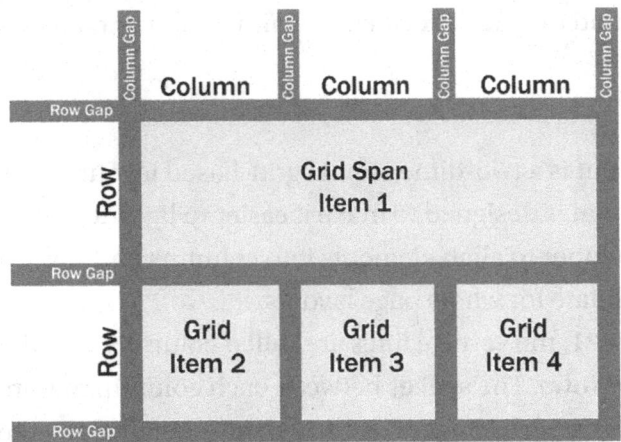

Figure 4-22. *CSS Grid with Items*

Putting CSS Grid into Practice

In this example, we want to lay out our website as follows. We want the width to span four columns. This means the header and the footer will span the full four columns. We also want the content to fill three columns (col 1, col 2, col 3). The sidebar will take up the last column (col 4). The site will also be split into three rows. The header on row 1, the content and sidebar on row 2, and the footer on row 3. We can see this layout in Figure 4-23.

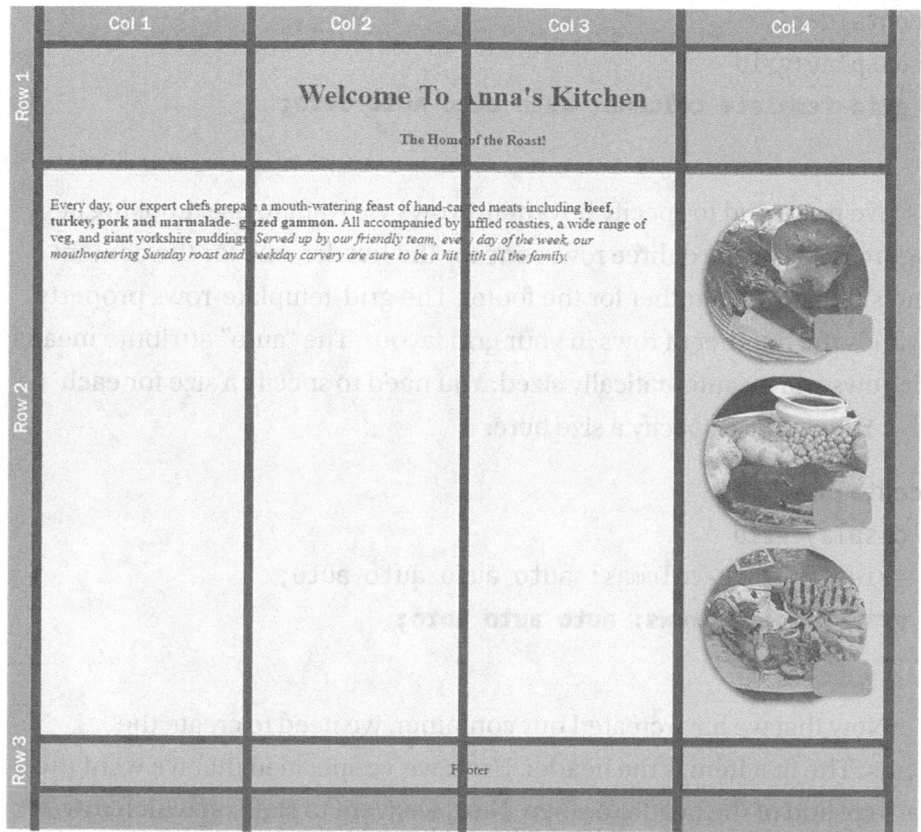

Figure 4-23. *CSS Grid Template*

First, we need to create a grid container:

```
.container {
  display:grid
}
```

Next, we need to specify how many rows and columns we are going to use. Looking at the template in Figure 4-23, we need four columns. The grid-template-columns property defines the number of columns in your grid layout. The "auto" attribute means the columns will be automatically sized. You need to specify a size for each column. You can also specify a size here:

```
.container {
  display:grid
  grid-template-columns: auto auto auto auto;
}
```

We now need to specify how many rows we want to use. Looking at Figure 4-23, we need three rows: one for the header, one for the content and sidebar, and another for the footer. The grid-template-rows property defines the number of rows in your grid layout. The "auto" attribute means the rows will be automatically sized. You need to specify a size for each row. You can also specify a size here:

```
.container {
  display:grid
  grid-template-columns: auto auto auto auto;
  grid-template-rows: auto auto auto;
}
```

Now that we have created our container, we need to create the items. The first item is the header. Here, we've specified that we want the background of the header orange. Next, we want to state on which row/column the header starts:

```
grid-row-start: 1;
grid-column-start: 1;
```

Here, we're starting on row 1, column 1, and the header ends before row 2, column 5. For this, we use the grid-row-end property. This defines how many rows an item will span or on which row line the item will end:

```
grid-row-end: 2;
grid-column-end: 5;
```

We end up with this:

```
.header {
    background-color: orange;
    grid-row-start: 1;
    grid-column-start: 1;
    grid-row-end: 2;
    grid-column-end: 5;
    padding: 20px;
    text-align: center;
}
```

Finally, we can add some padding to space out the contents of the header and align the text to the center.

We can do the same for the footer. Here, the footer starts on row 3 and ends after column 4 (which is 5). Again, we change the background color to orange and add some padding with the text aligned to the center:

```
.footer {
    background-color: orange;
    grid-row-start: 3;
    grid-column-start: 1;
    grid-row-end: 4;
    grid-column-end: 5;
    padding: 20px;
    text-align: center;
}
```

Now, for the content, this will start on row 2, but only span columns 1, 2, and 3 – so we end after 3 (which is 4). The sidebar will fill the last column:

```
.content {
    grid-row-start: 2;
    grid-column-start: 1;
```

```
  grid-row-end: 3;
  grid-column-end: 4;
  padding: 20px;
}
```

For the sidebar, we want to start on row 2, but just fill the last column after the content, so we start on column 4 and end after column 4 (which is 5):

```
.sidebar {
  background-color: lightgrey;
  grid-row-start: 2;
  grid-column-start: 4;
  grid-row-end: 3;
  grid-column-end: 5;
}
```

Now we need to build the page using the grid containers in our HTML document. We do this with the <div> tag.

First, we add the container; remember we called the container layout-grid and it's specified as a class, so we add it using the class attribute to the opening <div> tag:

```
<div class="layout-grid">
```

Inside, we can add the elements. First is the header:

```
<div class="header">
  <h1> Welcome To Anna's Kitchen</h1>
  <b> The Home of the Roast! </b>
</div>
```

then the rest of the elements. Just add the contents to the elements between the two <div> tags:

```
<div class="content">
    ...
</div>
```

```
<div class="sidebar">
   ...
</div>
<div class="footer">
   ...
</div>
</div>
```

Let's put it all together and see what it looks like (Figure 4-24).

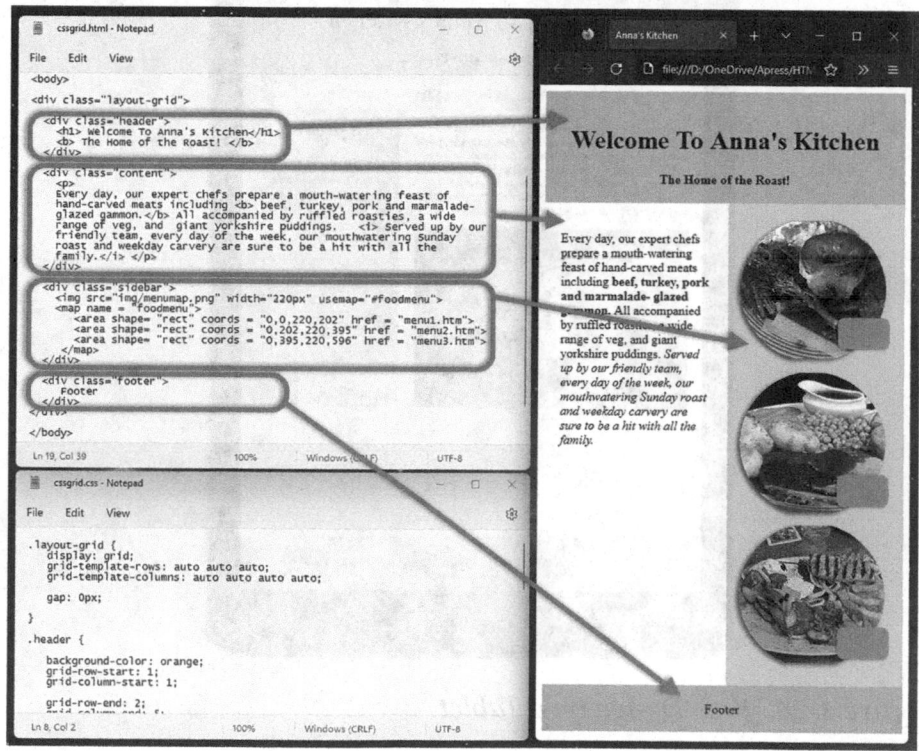

Figure 4-24. *Elements Added*

Responsive Grid Layouts

Responsive design is an approach to web design that allows your website content to adapt to different screen and window sizes used on a variety of different devices such as phones, tablets, and computers.

If we have a look at a simple website on a tablet, the screen looks OK and is sized correctly (Figure 4-25).

Figure 4-25. *Web Design on a Tablet*

Notice what happens when you resize the browser window on the PC. The layout starts to stretch and resize. You can see that the background image in the sidebar on the right no longer fits and is too small (Figure 4-26).

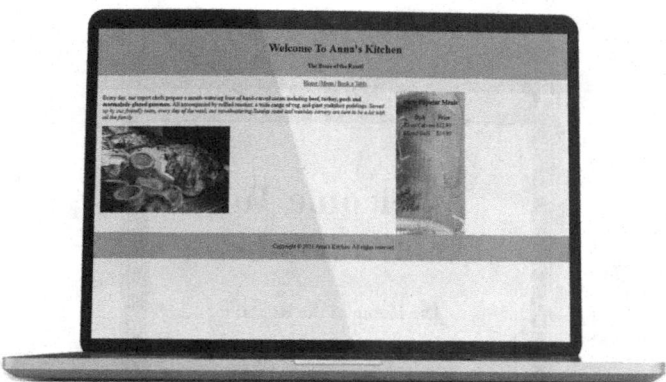

Figure 4-26. *Web Design on a Laptop*

Or if we view the website on a phone (Figure 4-27), the sidebar is hidden below the main text.

Figure 4-27. *Web Design on a Phone*

The layout changes depending on the screen size. Pages should be optimized for a variety of screen sizes, but how do we do this? These days, thanks to smartphones, tablets, laptops with different screen sizes, and PCs, many web pages are based on a responsive grid view. This means web pages based on a grid view are divided into columns.

A responsive grid view often has 12 columns and has a total width of 100%. This will shrink or expand as you resize the browser window (Figure 4-28).

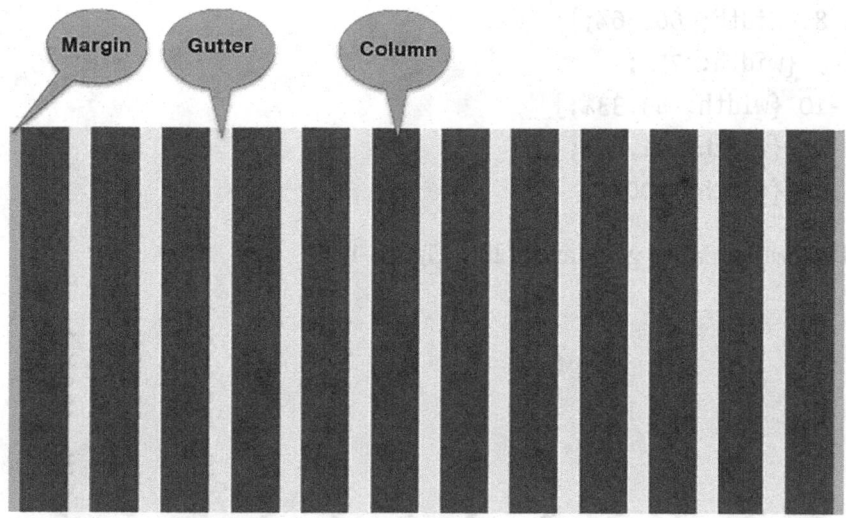

Figure 4-28. *Responsive Grid View*

Between each column, you'll find a gutter, and at either side of the grid, there is a margin.

To construct the grid view in CSS, first we calculate the percentage for one column:

100% / 12 **x 1** columns = 8.33%.

The next column would be 100% / 12 **x 2** = 16.66%.

The next column: 100% / 12 **x 3** = 25%.

And so on....

Next, we need to make one class for each of the 12 columns and the percentage sizes we calculated in the previous step:

```
.col-1 {width: 8.33%;}
.col-2 {width: 16.66%;}
.col-3 {width: 25%;}
.col-4 {width: 33.33%;}
.col-5 {width: 41.66%;}
.col-6 {width: 50%;}
.col-7 {width: 58.33%;}
```

```
.col-8 {width: 66.66%;}
.col-9 {width: 75%;}
.col-10 {width: 83.33%;}
.col-11 {width: 91.66%;}
.col-12 {width: 100%;}
```

This will create a grid layout like Figure 4-29.

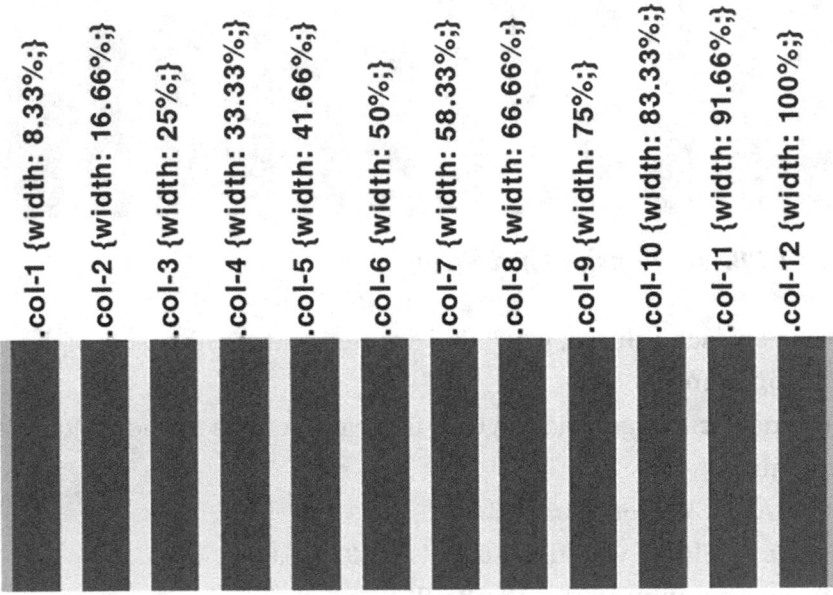

Figure 4-29. Responsive Grid View Showing Column Widths

Remember the CSS file we built in the previous section. Padding and borders should be included in the total width and height of the elements. To enforce this, we add the following to the top of the CSS file:

```
* {
  box-sizing: border-box;
}
```

We can add the column declarations to the bottom of the CSS file:

```
.col-1 {width: 8.33%;}
.col-2 {width: 16.66%;}
.col-3 {width: 25%;}
.col-4 {width: 33.33%;}
.col-5 {width: 41.66%;}
.col-6 {width: 50%;}
.col-7 {width: 58.33%;}
.col-8 {width: 66.66%;}
.col-9 {width: 75%;}
.col-10 {width: 83.33%;}
.col-11 {width: 91.66%;}
.col-12 {width: 100%;}
```

Now we can build the page using HTML. We can add the header and nav bar. These two sections will span 100% across the page:

```
<header>
    <h1> Welcome To Anna's Kitchen</h1>

    <b> The Home of the Roast! </b>
</header>

<nav>
    <a href="index.html"> Home </a> |
    <a href="menu.html"> Menu </a> |
    <a href="menu.html"> Book a Table </a>
</nav>
```

Next, let's add the content and sidebar. Now for this section, we want the content section to span eight columns across and the sidebar to span the remaining four columns:

```
<content class="col-8">
    <p>
```

117

```
Every day, our expert chefs prepare a mouth-watering
... </p>
<img src="img/carvery.jpg" width="365px">
</content>
```

You can see the main content will span eight columns as shown in Figure 4-30.

Figure 4-30. *Responsive Grid View for the Main Content*

After that, we can add the sidebar:

```
<sidebar class="col-4">
    <h3 align="center">Most Popular Meals</h3>
    <table align="center">
      <tr>
        <th>Dish</th>
```

118

```
        <th>Price</th>
      </tr>
      <tr>
        <td>Roast Carvery</td>
        <td>$12.99</td>
      </tr>
      <tr>
        <td>Mixed Grill</td>
        <td>$14.99</td>
    </tr>
  </table>
</sidebar>
```

This spans four columns as we can see in Figure 4-31.

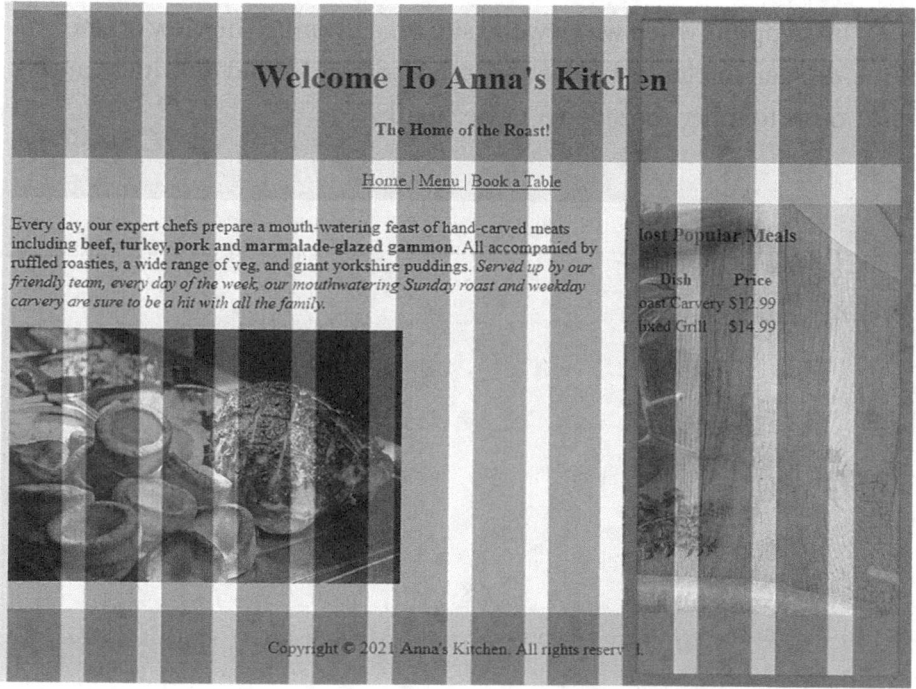

Figure 4-31. *Responsive Grid View for the Sidebar*

Now what happens when you resize the browser window? You'll see the content stretch to fill the screen (Figure 4-32).

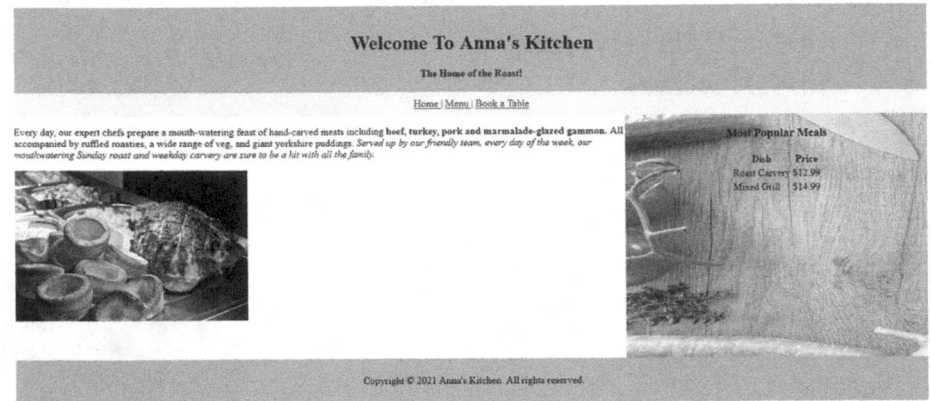

Figure 4-32. *The Content Stretched to Fill the Screen*

What happens when we view the site on a phone? The view on the phone, as seen in Figure 4-33, is a bit cramped and could do with some breakpoints to move the sidebar underneath.

Figure 4-33. *A Cramped View on a Phone*

To do this, we must understand what a viewport is. The viewport is the portion of the website that the user can see (Figure 4-34).

Figure 4-34. *Viewport*

A meta viewport tag gives the browser instructions on how to control the page's dimensions and scaling (Figure 4-35):

```
<meta name="viewport" content="width=device-width, initial-scale=1">
```

Using the meta viewport value, **width=device-width** instructs the page to match the screen's width in device-independent pixels. The **initial-scale=1.0** part sets the initial zoom level when the page is first loaded by the browser.

To provide the best experience, mobile browsers render the page at a desktop screen of about 767–980px in width and then scale the content by increasing font sizes and resizing the content to fit the screen.

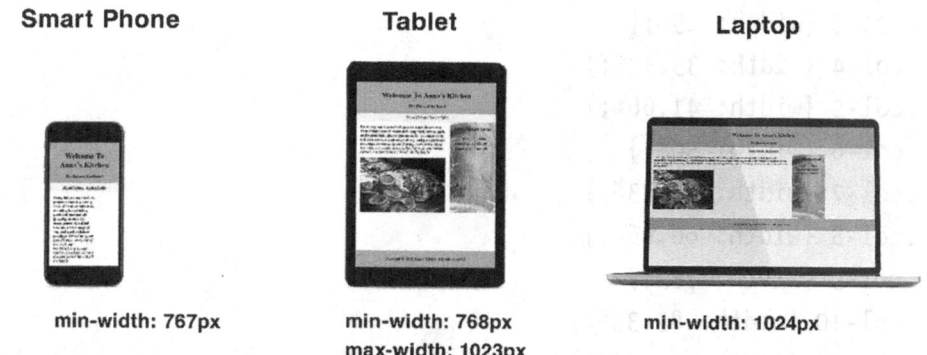

Figure 4-35. *The Website on Different Screen Sizes*

Media queries make it possible to respond to a client browser with a customized display for certain viewport sizes. The @media rule includes a block of CSS properties only if a certain condition is true.

Going back to our CSS, we can style all column widths to span 100% of the width on smartphone devices with small screens. The following code selects any element that contains **"col-"** anywhere in the value of the class attribute:

```
[class*="col-"] {
  width: 100%;
}
```

This is known as a CSS attribute selector with the attribute we want to select enclosed in square brackets [].

Here's the media query to deal with larger screens. The min-width media property specifies the minimum width of a specific device. So the screen width needs to be 768px or greater. This would work well on larger tablets such as an iPad or a laptop.

```
@media only screen and (min-width: 768px) {
  .col-1 {width: 8.33%;}
  .col-2 {width: 16.66%;}
```

```
        .col-3 {width: 25%;}
        .col-4 {width: 33.33%;}
        .col-5 {width: 41.66%;}
        .col-6 {width: 50%;}
        .col-7 {width: 58.33%;}
        .col-8 {width: 66.66%;}
        .col-9 {width: 75%;}
        .col-10 {width: 83.33%;}
        .col-11 {width: 91.66%;}
        .col-12 {width: 100%;}
}
```

This creates a breakpoint when the browser window is 768px wide.

You can set your breakpoints using min-width and max-width properties. When should you use each one? Well, if you are designing your layout for small smartphone screens first, then use min-width breakpoints and work your way up. If you've designed the website for a desktop display first, and you want to adapt the layout for smaller screens, then use max-width and work your way down to the smallest screen.

Lab Exercises

1. What is CSS?

2. How do you include CSS in your HTML document? Describe the three methods.

3. What is a selector? What are the different types and what do they do?

4. Create a new HTML file and name it ch04.html.

5. Create a new CSS file and name it ch04.css.

6. In the file ch04.html, add the basic structure of an HTML document.

7. Link the CSS file ch04.css in your HTML document.

8. What is the difference between absolute and relative measurements?

9. Name some absolute measurement units.

10. Name some relative measurement units.

Summary

- Cascading Style Sheets (CSS) are used to define and customize the styles and layouts for your web pages.

- Can be included inline within an HTML element.

- Can be included from an external file using <script href= "">.

- Can be included in an HTML file itself between <script> ... </script> tags.

- A type selector creates a general style for the declared element.

- A class selector is used to apply styles to a specific HTML element and is referenced using a dot.

- The ID selector targets a single element and can only be used once per page and is referenced using a hash.

- The universal selector matches every single element on the page and is referenced using an asterisk.

- Specify colors using a keyword, a hex value, or an RGB value.

- Use inch, millimeter, px, or pt for specifying absolute measurements.

- Use em or a percentage for specifying relative measurements.

- Flexbox is a layout module designed for laying out groups of items in one dimension (using a row or column, but not both at the same time).

- A CSS grid is a two-dimensional layout feature and is a perfect candidate for whole page layouts (using rows and columns).

CHAPTER 5

Special Effects

Using HTML and CSS, you can add various effects to decorate your website. These include

- Hover effects

- Buttons

- Rounded corners

- Shadows

- Gradients

These effects should be used sparingly as they can become irritating and distracting if used in abundance.

However, effects can be useful to add emphasis to a section or object.

Text Effects

In this example, we are going to add a shadow effect to a heading. Using CSS, we can style the heading using the text-shadow property:

```
h1 {
  text-shadow: 2px 2px 2px lightgrey;
}
```

© Kevin Wilson 2023
K. Wilson, *The Absolute Beginner's Guide to HTML and CSS*,
https://doi.org/10.1007/978-1-4842-9250-1_5

We can also change the text to white using the color property:

```
h1 {
  color: white;
  text-shadow: 2px 2px 2px lightgrey;
}
```

Let's take a look at an example. Here, we've added a text-shadow property to the heading 1 selector as you can see in the about.css file (Figure 5-1).

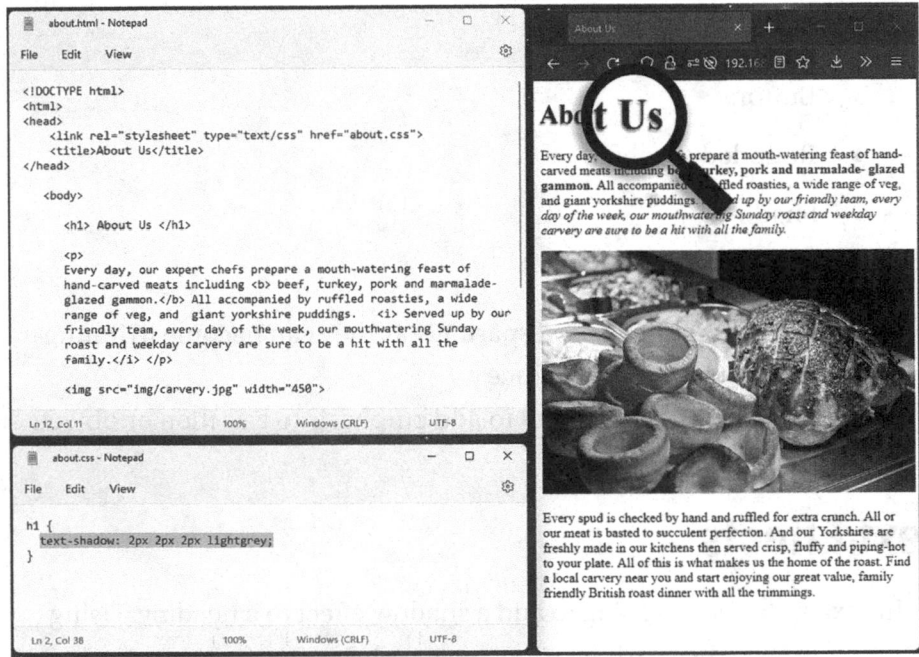

Figure 5-1. *Text Shadow Property*

In the web browser on the right in Figure 5-1, you can see the shadow around the heading.

Rounded Image Corners

We can style images. We can round the corners of the image. The amount of curve on the corner is called the border radius:

```
img {
  border-radius: 10px;
}
```

Let's take a look at an example. Here, we've added a border-radius property to the img selector as you can see in the about.css file in Figure 5-2.

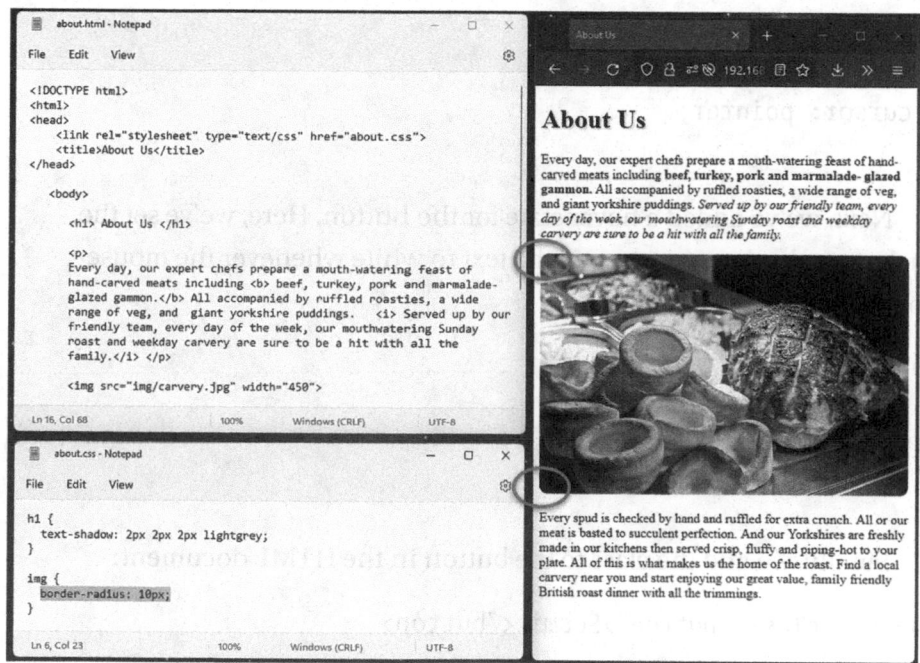

Figure 5-2. *Rounded Corners*

You can see the rounded corners of the photo in the browser window in Figure 5-2.

Buttons

We add styles to buttons. Here, we've created a button class selector. We've set the background color of the button to orange, the text to white, plus we've added rounded corners using the border-radius property. We've also added a property to change the mouse pointer to a hand pointer using the cursor property:

```
.button {
  background-color: orange;
  color: white;
  border: none;
  border-radius: 4px;
  padding: 15px 25px;
  cursor: pointer;
}
```

Next, we've added a hover state for the button. Here, we've set the background color to green and the text to white whenever the mouse pointer hovers over the button:

```
.button:hover {
  background-color: green;
  color: white;
}
```

Finally, we add the class to the button in the HTML document:

```
<button class="button">Submit</button>
```

Let's take a look. At the bottom of the page in the web browser, you'll see the button change color and the cursor change to a hand pointer when you hover your mouse pointer over the button (Figure 5-3).

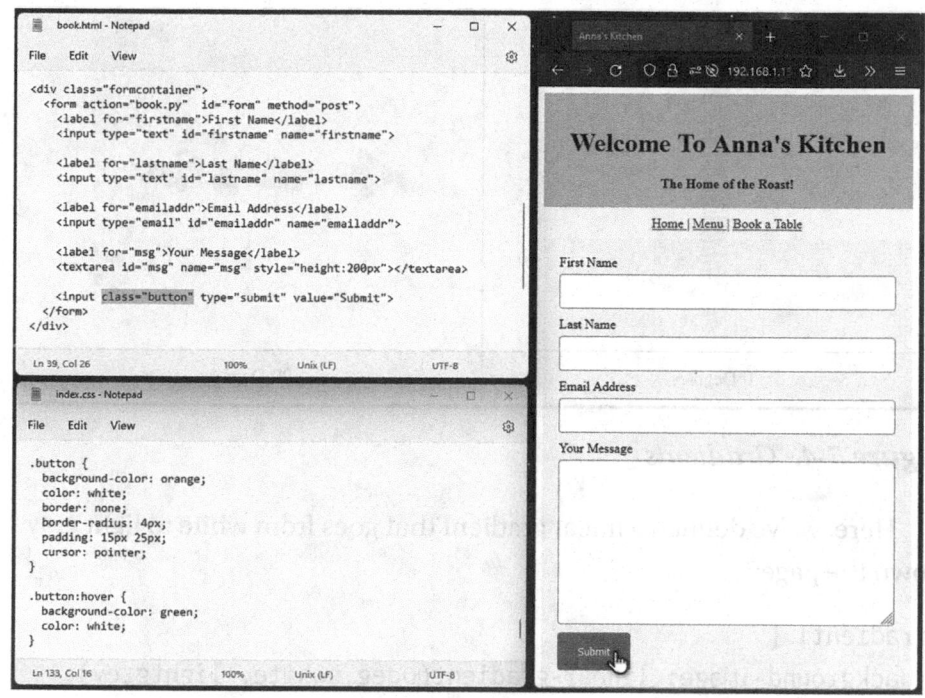

Figure 5-3. *The Cursor Changes*

Gradients

You can add gradients to your page (Figure 5-4). A gradient is a smooth transition between two or more specified colors.

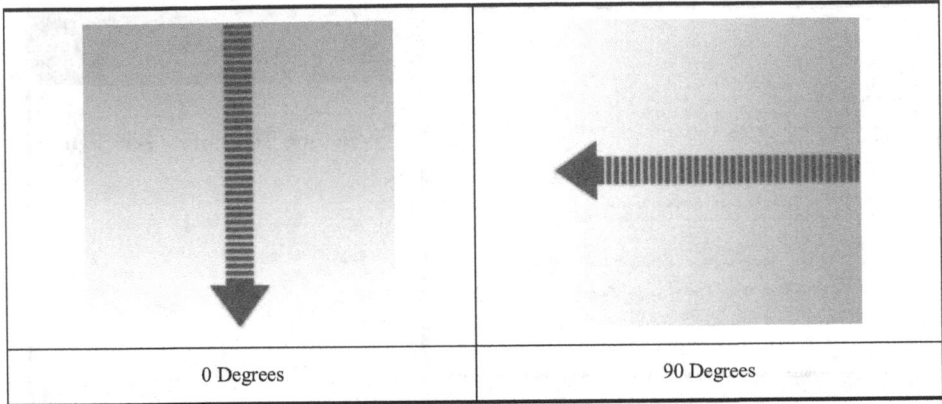

Figure 5-4. *Gradients*

Here, we've defined a linear gradient that goes from white to light gray down the page:

```
#gradient1 {
  background-image: linear-gradient(0deg, white, lightgrey);
}
```

Now anything we want the gradient to span, we enclose in <div> tags:

```
<div id="gradient1" style="text-align:center;">

...

</div>
```

Let's take a look at an example. In Figure 5-5, we've defined a gradient ID selector. We've added a gradient spanning from light gray to white down the page (0 degrees).

We've also enclosed the text between the <div> tags, so we know where the gradient will start and where it will end.

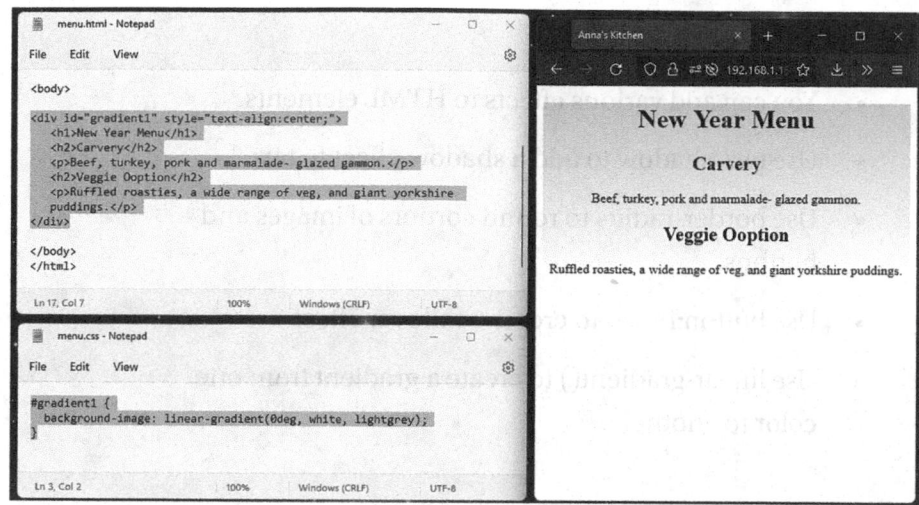

Figure 5-5. *Gradients in Use*

Lab Exercises

1. What is CSS?

2. What is a selector? What are the different types and what do they do?

3. Create a new HTML file and name it ch05.html.

4. Create a new CSS file and name it ch05.css.

5. In the file ch05.html, add the basic structure of an HTML document.

6. Link the CSS file ch04.css in your HTML document.

Summary

- You can add various effects to HTML elements.

- Use text-shadow to add a shadow effect to text.

- Use border-radius to round corners of images and buttons.

- Use button:hover to create a rollover effect.

- Use linear-gradient() to create a gradient from one color to another.

CHAPTER 6

Multimedia

Using the HTML5 specification, it is a lot easier to embed multimedia into your website. You can easily embed video, music, animations, and sound.

Multimedia files have various file extensions.

Audio files can be .wav, .mp3, .aac, or .wma.

Video files can be .mp4, .mpg, .wmv, .webm, or .avi.

Photos and illustrations are usually .jpg, .png, or .webp.

Adding Video

Use the built-in <video>...</video> tags:

```
<video width="450" controls autoplay>
    <source src="video.mp4" type="video/mp4">
</video>
```

Use the source attribute to specify the video file and format. You can list multiple formats here, but H264 "MP4" and WEBM seem to be the most popular.

Use the width attribute to set the width of the video window or use the height attribute to set the height. Note, if you want to maintain the aspect ratio of the video, you only need to specify one of the two attributes: width or height. This prevents the video getting stretched or squashed. You can also specify a percentage, for example, 100%, to span the video across the whole page regardless of the browser window size – this is sometimes useful if you are developing for different screen sizes.

© Kevin Wilson 2023
K. Wilson, *The Absolute Beginner's Guide to HTML and CSS*,
https://doi.org/10.1007/978-1-4842-9250-1_6

If you want controls such as play, stop, and skip to appear along the bottom of your video window, add the attribute "controls"; if not, leave the attribute out.

If you want the video to automatically start when the page loads, add the attribute "autoplay." Browsers tend to block this feature, and most videos won't start to play unless the user clicks the play button.

Try adding the code to your index.html file (Figure 6-1) and see what happens.

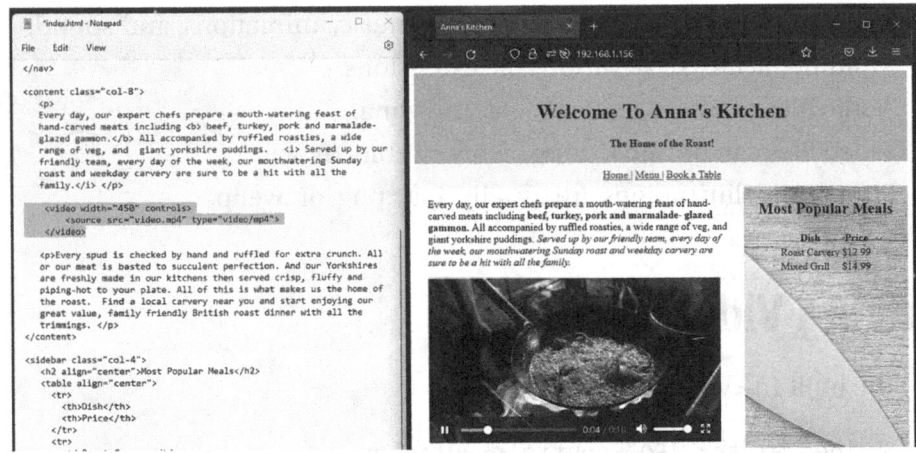

Figure 6-1. *Embedding a Video*

If you upload video files to your web server, you'll need to have plenty of space to store the files as well as enough bandwidth to transfer the video to whomever visits your website.

Another method is to upload your video file to a video hosting service such as YouTube or Vimeo. That way, your video is streamed to the user's device rather than downloaded first.

In Figure 6-2, I've uploaded my video to Vimeo.

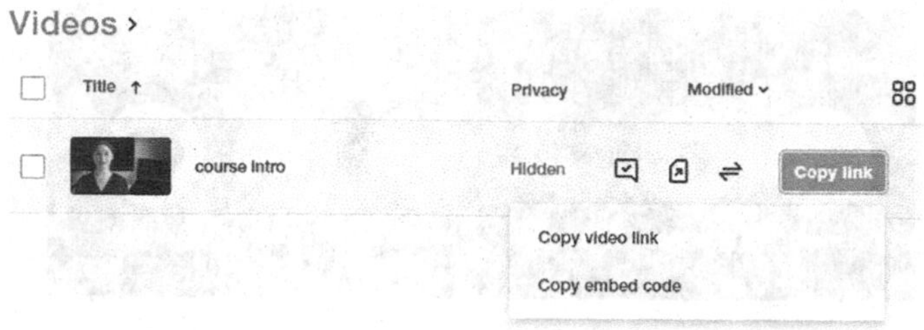

Figure 6-2. *Vimeo Upload*

All you need to do is copy the video's embed code and paste it into your HTML code:

```
<iframe
    src="https://player.vimeo.com/video/738226502?h=1d66dead64"
    width="450"
    height="220"
    frameborder="0"
    allow="autoplay;
    fullscreen" allowfullscreen>
</iframe>
```

If you are using YouTube, once you've uploaded your video, you'll need to copy the embed code. To do this, select "share" at the bottom of the video on YouTube (Figure 6-3).

Figure 6-3. *The YouTube Share Button*

From the pop-up dialog box, select embed (Figure 6-4).

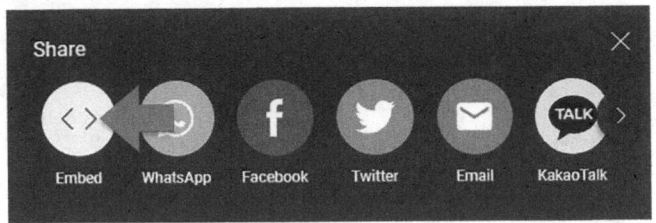

Figure 6-4. *Embed*

Click copy on the bottom right of the screen (Figure 6-5).

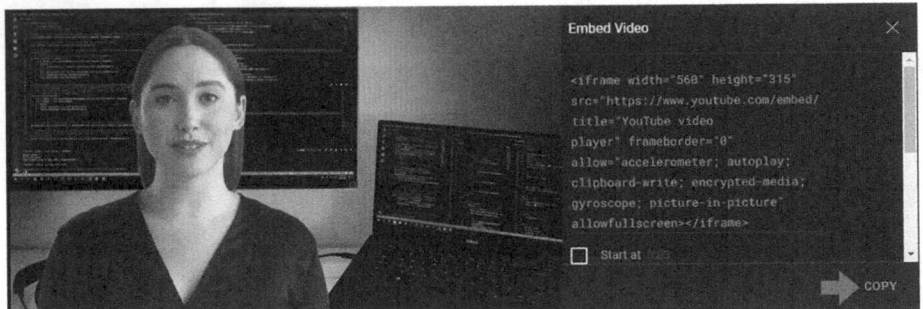

Figure 6-5. *Copy the Code*

Paste the code into your HTML document at the position you want the video to appear. I'm going to paste the video after the first paragraph (Figure 6-6).

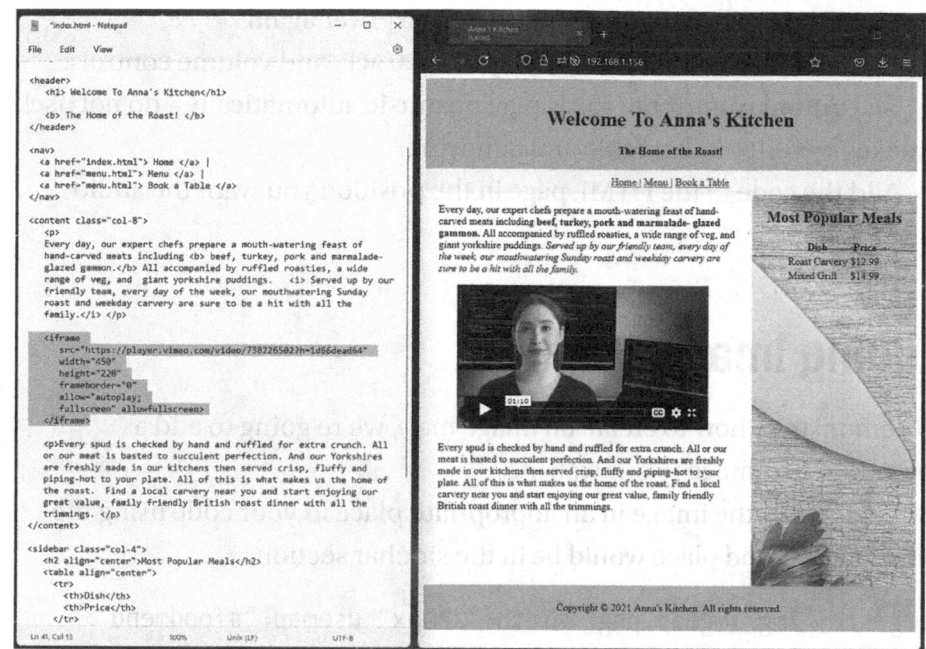

Figure 6-6. *The Video in the Website*

You can adjust the size using the width and height attributes. You can also add or remove the frame and allow autoplay and fullscreen modes.

Adding Audio

If you are adding background music or any sound to your website, make sure it is appropriate and complements the website. There is nothing worse than going to a website and have annoying music or sound blaring at you.

To add audio, use the <audio>…</audio> tags:

```
<audio controls>
    <source src= "music.mp3" type= "audio/mpeg">
</audio>
```

The **loop** attribute loops the music to play over again.

The **controls** attribute shows play, stop, track, and volume controls.

The **autoplay** attribute starts playing music automatically – do not use! It makes websites unbearable and annoying.

Add the code to the HTML page in the position you want the audio player to appear.

Adding Image Maps

To demonstrate how to create an image map, we're going to add a navigation bar image to our website.

First, insert the image in an appropriate place in your code using the <img> tag. A good place would be in the sidebar section:

```
<img src="img/imgmap.png" width="220px" usemap="#foodmenu">
```

Add the usemap attribute and add the image map name.

Now to create an image map, use the <map>...</map> tags. Give the map a name using the name attribute. This needs to match the usemap attribute in the <img> tag you added earlier:

```
<map name = "foodmenu">
  <area shape= "rect" coords = "0,0,0,0"
      href = "menu.htm">
</map>
```

Inside the <map>...</map> tags, you need to define hotspots around parts of the image you want the user to click.

You need to create these hotspots using a coordinate system (coords = "x,y,x,y"). This corresponds to x&y coordinates of the top left and the x&y coordinates of the bottom right of the hotspot within the image dimensions.

To find these coordinates and the image dimensions, you'll need an image editor. You can download GIMP which is a great free alternative to Photoshop. GIMP has a pixel measuring tool which is quite useful for this task.

`www.gimp.org/downloads/`

Click "Download GIMP directly."

Load the image into GIMP. The image needs to be the same size as it is in the HTML document, so you'll need to resize if necessary. In this example, we set the width of the image to 220px in our HTML code.

Our sidebar is 220px wide (x) by 598px long (y) (Figure 6-7).

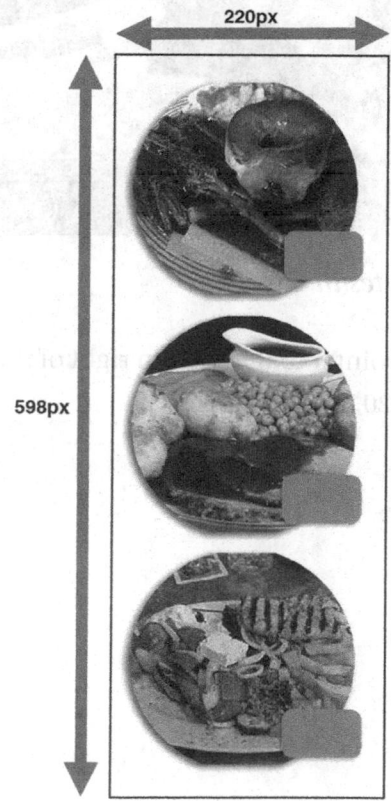

Figure 6-7. *Resizing the Image*

We need to divide the image into three sections. The first image is the first hotspot on the image map, the second image is the second hotspot, and the third image is the third hotspot.

To find these using GIMP, hover your mouse over the image. You'll see a set of coordinates in the bottom-left corner of the screen (Figure 6-8).

Figure 6-8. *Coordinates in GIMP*

Move your mouse pointer to the bottom right of the first image and note the coordinates (220, 202) in Figure 6-9.

Figure 6-9. *Coordinates of the First Image*

We can add this value to the image map:

```
<map name = "foodmenu">
  <area shape= "rect" coords = "0,0,220,202"
      href = "menu.htm">
</map>
```

Do the same for the other two images (Figure 6-10).

Figure 6-10. *Image Coordinates*

You'll end up with something like this:

```
<img src="img/menumap.png" width="220px" usemap="#foodmenu">
```

```
<map name = "foodmenu">
  <area shape= "rect" coords = "0,0,220,202" href =
  "menu1.htm">
  <area shape= "rect" coords = "0,202,220,395" href =
  "menu2.htm">
  <area shape= "rect" coords = "0,395,220,596" href =
  "menu3.htm">
</map>
```

Now when you click the image in the sidebar, you'll be taken to the HTML page specified in the href attribute (Figure 6-11).

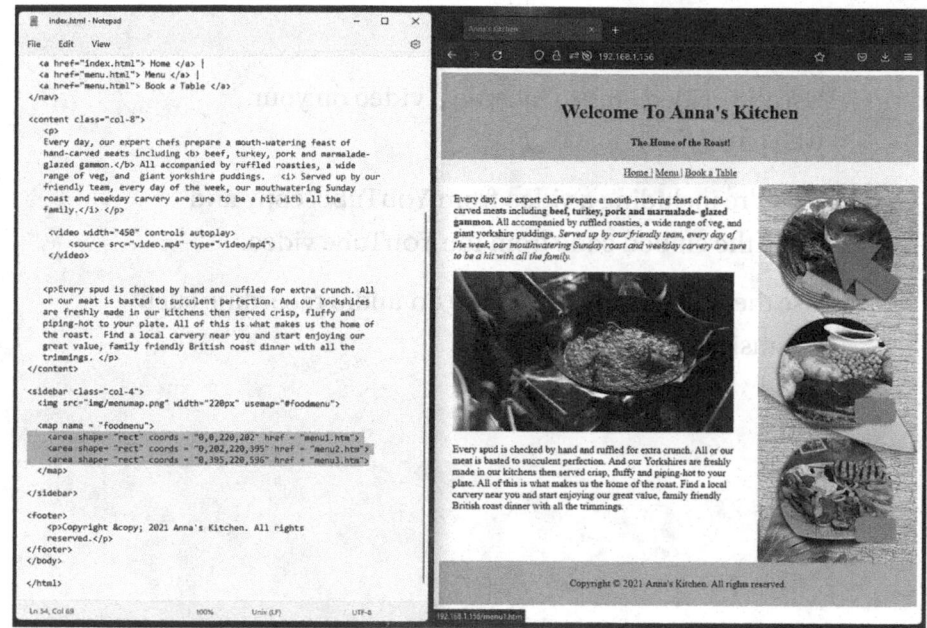

Figure 6-11. *The Final Result*

Lab Exercises

1. Create a new HTML file.

2. Where do you store video and audio files to be included on a web page?

3. Add a video from YouTube or one of your own videos to the web page.

4. Underneath, add an MP3 audio recording.

Summary

- Use the <video> tag to include a video on your web page.

- If you're including a video from YouTube, copy and paste the embed code from the YouTube video.

- Use the <audio> tag to include an audio recording such as music or other audio.

CHAPTER 7

HTML Forms

A form is an HTML document used to collect user input (Figure 7-1). The information entered by the user is usually sent to a server and is processed by a script.

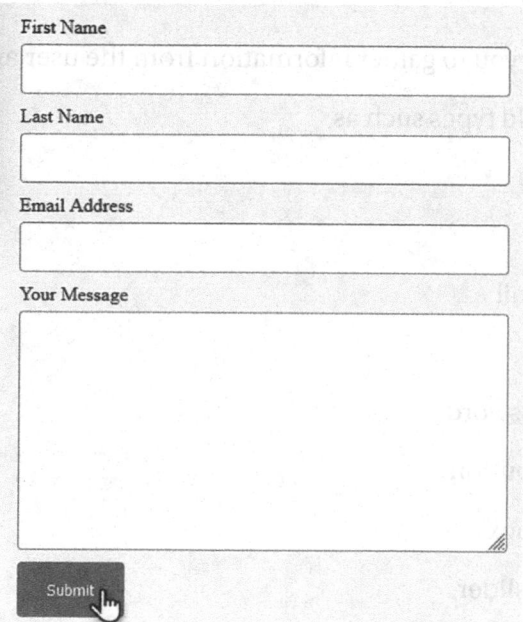

Figure 7-1. *A Form*

An HTML form contains fields for name, password, telephone number, and email address, as well as larger fields to capture messages. You can also add radio buttons, select boxes, and a submit button.

© Kevin Wilson 2023
K. Wilson, *The Absolute Beginner's Guide to HTML and CSS*,
https://doi.org/10.1007/978-1-4842-9250-1_7

Adding Forms

Forms provide a way to acquire information from the user.

Use the tags:

```
<form action=" ">...</form>
```

Use the action attribute to point to a PHP or CGI script to process the inputted data.

Inside the <form> tags, you need to add some input elements.

Input Types

Input types allow you to gather information from the user and can be

- Text field types such as

  - text

  - tel

  - email

  - url

  - password

- Radio button

- Checkbox

- Range slider

- Button

  - submit

  - reset

- File

Use the <input> element to define your input types:

```
<input type = " " name = " ">... </input>
```

The type attribute indicates the type of input such as text field, radio button, checkbox, etc.

The name attribute specifies the name of an <input> element and can be referenced in a JavaScript or to identify the inputted data after a form is submitted for processing.

You can also add an id attribute that assigns an identifier that allows a JavaScript or CSS ID selector to easily access the <input> element.

Text Fields

A text field is an input type and can accept text, telephone numbers, email addresses, or passwords. Each field type is preset to expect a certain format and type of text. For example, the email type expects to find an @ sign entered indicating an email address. A password type masks the letters with *** as you type them in.

```
<input type="text" name="firstname"> </input>
```

Text Area

This is a text field that will allow multiple lines of text and is best used when accepting paragraphs of text such as a message on a contact form (Figure 7-2):

```
<textarea name= "message" rows= "5" cols= "30">
   ...
</textarea>
```

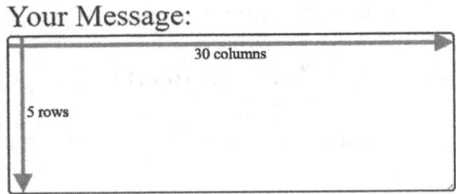

Figure 7-2. *A Message*

Radio Buttons

These allow the user to select from preset options:

```
<input type= "radio" name= "gender" value= "female">
  </input>
```

For example, see Figure 7-3.

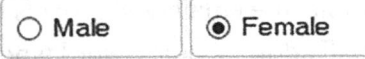

Figure 7-3. *A Radio Button*

Checkbox

This creates a set of options for the user to choose from (Figure 7-4):

```
<input type="checkbox" name="mainoption1" value="Starter">
<label for=" mainoption1"> I will have a starter</label>
```

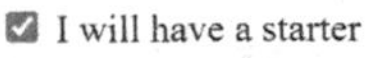

☑ I will have a starter

Figure 7-4. *A Checkbox*

150

Select List

This creates a drop-down list of preset options for the user to choose from (Figure 7-5):

```
<select>
    <option value= "US">United States</option>
    <option value= "UK">United Kingdom</option>
    <option value= "EU">Europe</option>
</select>
```

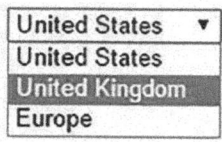

Figure 7-5. *A Drop-Down List*

Labels

Labels are used to label the fields in your form (Figure 7-6):

```
<label for = "name"> Name: </label>
```

Name: [   ]

Figure 7-6. *A Label*

The "for" attribute must match the name of the field you're labeling. For example, the preceding label is labeling the following text field:

```
<input type= "text" name= "name" width= "350"> </input>
```

Submit Button

The submit button sends all form values to a form handler which is usually a server-side script:

```
<input type="submit" value="Submit">
```

or

```
<button type="submit">Submit</button>
```

You'll end up with something like Figure 7-7.

Figure 7-7. *A Submit Button*

Building a Form

Let's go back to our website project and create a table booking form. Here, we've added some code to create our form.

The form code goes between the <form> tags in the HTML body. Inside the form tag, with the action attribute we specify the script we want to execute when the user clicks the submit button. This would be a PHP or Python script that is executed on the server (in this example, we'll use a PHP script). Set the send method to post and give the form an ID. See later.

```
<form action="book.php"  id="form" method="post">
```

Next, we've added a label for the name field followed by the input field itself. Inside the input field, set the type (text, email, or password), then give the field a name and ID:

```
<label for="firstname">First Name</label>
<input type="text" id="firstname" name="firstname">
```

Do the rest for the other fields.

The IDs are used later in the Python or PHP script that processes the form data.

We end up with something like Figure 7-8.

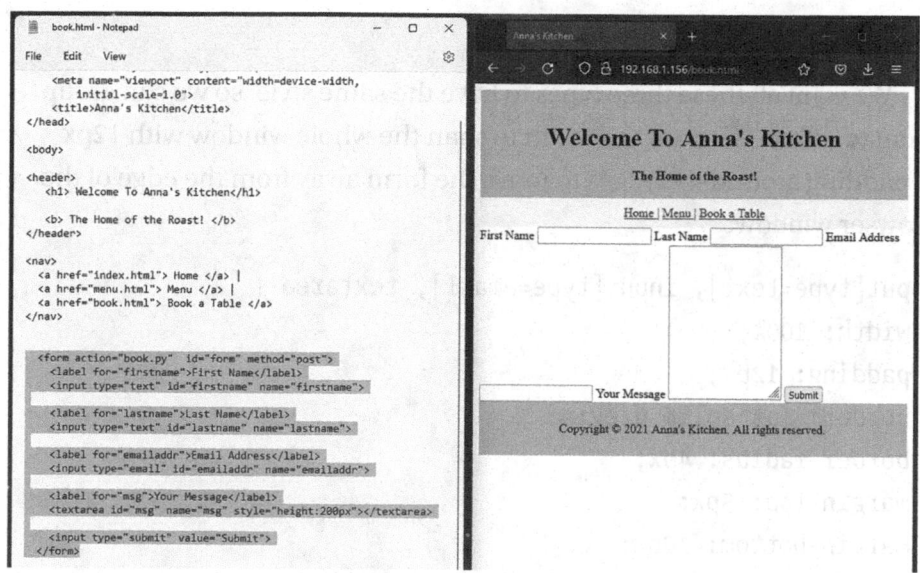

Figure 7-8. A Form in the Website

Styling a Form

Notice that the form looks a little rough. We can use our CSS selectors to style the form and make it look a little better.

To do this, we can add our CSS styles to our index.css file we were using in the previous chapters.

First, we need to style the input boxes. In this form, we have three different types of input box.

Input with plain text type

```
input[type=text]
```

153

Input with an email type (this checks for a valid email address)

```
input[type=email]
```

A large text field

```
textarea
```

We want all these three types to have the same style, so we can group them together. We want the width to span the whole window with 12px of padding around the edges to move the form away from the edge of the browser window:

```
input[type=text], input[type=email], textarea {
  width: 100%;
  padding: 12px;
  border: 1px solid grey;
  border-radius: 4px;
  margin-top: 5px;
  margin-bottom: 10px;
}
```

I've also added a thin border around each input field and colored it gray with a rounded edge (or border radius) on the corners.

I've added 5px at the top of each box (margin-top) and 10px below each box (margin-bottom) to separate them vertically on the form.

Next, we can style the submit button. We can do this with another input type:

```
input[type=submit] {
  background-color: orange;
  color: white;
  padding: 15px;
```

```
  border: none;
  border-radius: 4px;
  cursor: pointer;
}
```

To match the style of the website, I've changed the background color of the button to orange with white text.

I've also added 15px of padding around the inside of the button, removed the border, and added the 4px to border-radius to make the edges of the button rounded.

The property cursor: pointer changes your mouse pointer to a hand pointer when you hover your mouse over the button.

Finally, we need to create a container to hold the form. We can do this using the division <div> tag in the HTML code:

```
<div class="formcontainer">
```

We can style the form container in the CSS code like we did earlier:

```
.formcontainer {
  background-color: whitesmoke;
  padding: 20px;
}
```

Here, I've created a container with a gray background and a padding of 20px around the form to move it away from the rest of the page.

Once we've done that, we'll end up with something like Figure 7-9. Notice that the form looks a lot better.

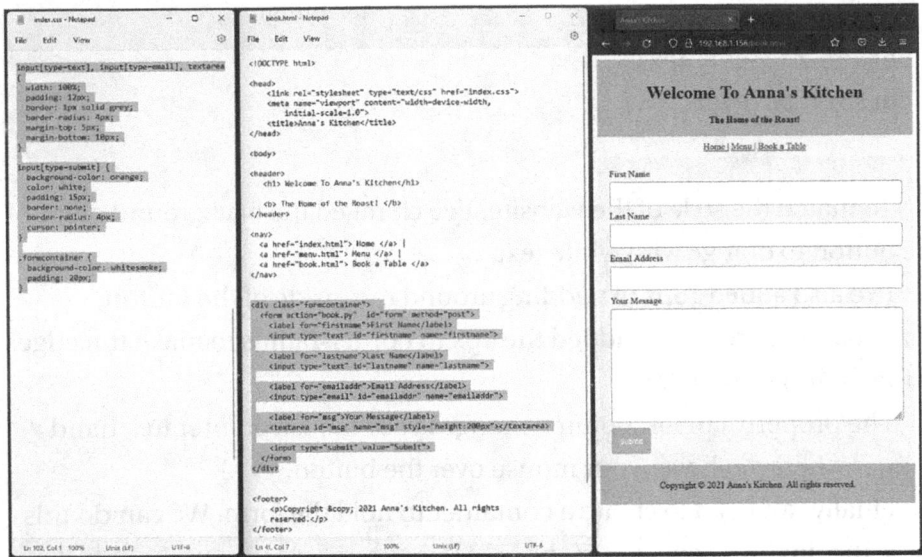

Figure 7-9. *A Formatted Form*

Processing the Form Data

Next, we need to add the functionality to the form (i.e., what happens when you click submit).

The form is usually processed on the server with a PHP or Python script and will take the details entered and send them to an email address. In this example, we are going to use a PHP script to process the form data.

Configure the Web Server to Execute Scripts

Now in order for this to work, you'll need PHP support installed on your web host (contact your hosting provider for details), or if you're using the Abyss Web Server we installed in Chapter 1, you'll need to install PHP scripting. To do this, go to the following website:

aprelium.com/downloads/

For Windows, download the preconfigured PHP package for Windows (64-bit) (Figure 7-10).

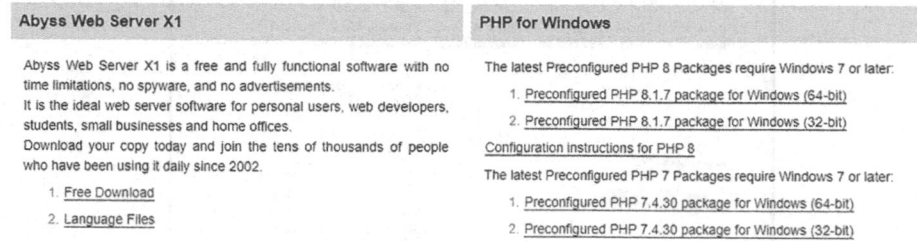

Abyss Web Server X1

Abyss Web Server X1 is a free and fully functional software with no time limitations, no spyware, and no advertisements.
It is the ideal web server software for personal users, web developers, students, small businesses and home offices.
Download your copy today and join the tens of thousands of people who have been using it daily since 2002.

1. Free Download
2. Language Files

PHP for Windows

The latest Preconfigured PHP 8 Packages require Windows 7 or later:
1. Preconfigured PHP 8.1.7 package for Windows (64-bit)
2. Preconfigured PHP 8.1.7 package for Windows (32-bit)
Configuration instructions for PHP 8
The latest Preconfigured PHP 7 Packages require Windows 7 or later:
1. Preconfigured PHP 7.4.30 package for Windows (64-bit)
2. Preconfigured PHP 7.4.30 package for Windows (32-bit)

Figure 7-10. *Installing PHP*

Go to your downloads folder, then double-click PHP8xx-x64.exe. Run through the setup and click "Next" to begin (Figure 7-11).

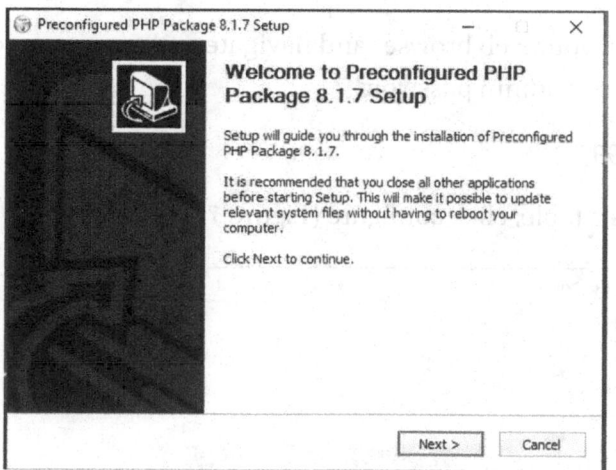

Figure 7-11. *Installing PHP*

Accept the license agreement, then click "Install." Make a note where the software is going to be installed (Figure 7-12), in this case, C:\Program Files\PHP8.

157

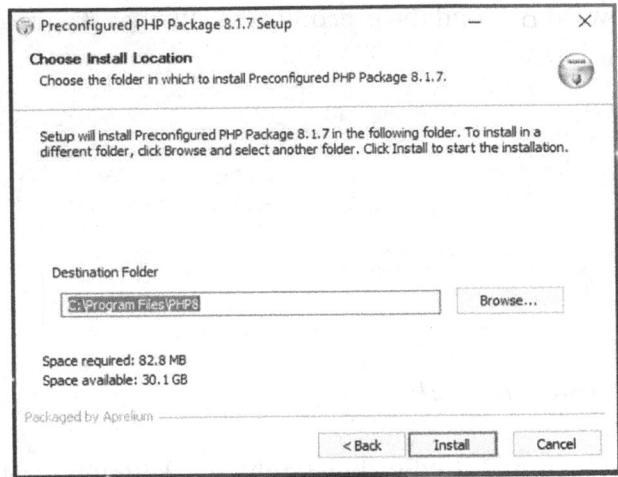

Figure 7-12. *Choosing Where to Install*

Next, open your web browser and navigate to the server's console. Enter the server's admin password.

`127.0.0.1:9999`

In the hosts table, click configure (Figure 7-13).

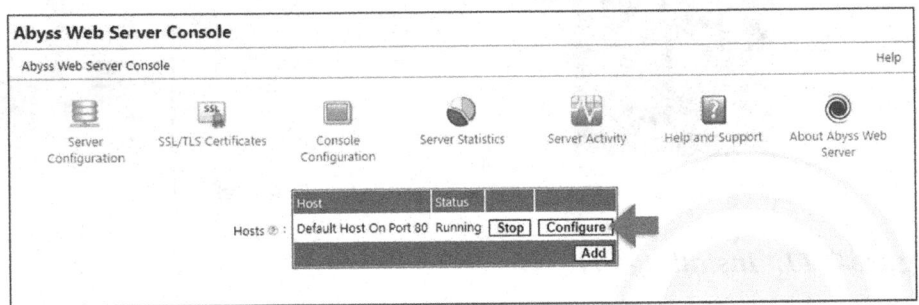

Figure 7-13. *Configuring the Console*

158

Select Scripting Parameters (Figure 7-14).

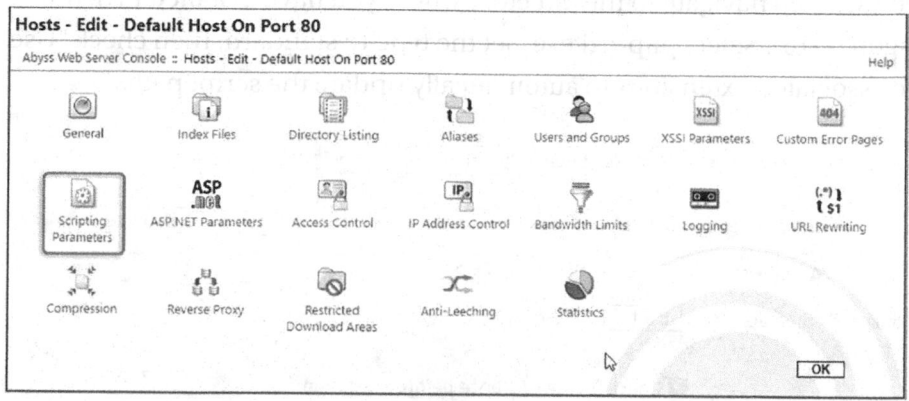

Figure 7-14. *Scripting Parameters*

Check Enable Scripts Execution, then click add in the Interpreters table (Figure 7-15).

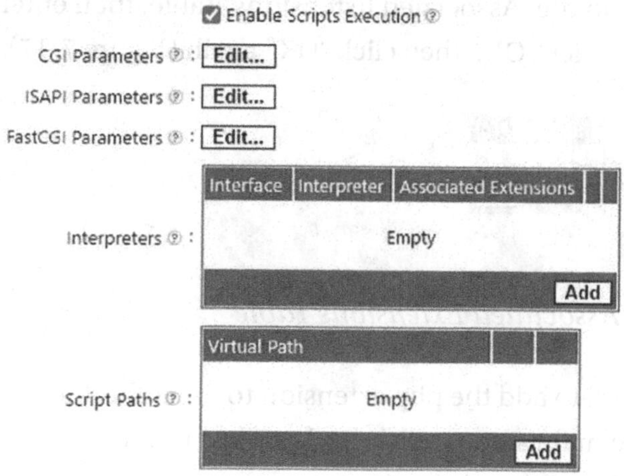

Figure 7-15. *Interpreters Table*

Set Interface to FastCGI (Local – Pipes). In the Interpreter field, click browse, then navigate to the directory where you have installed PHP 8 (Figure 7-16). Select php-cgi.exe. Set the type to standard, then check "Use the associated extensions to automatically update the script paths."

Interface ⑦ : [FastCGI (Local - Pipes)   ⌄]

Interpreter ⑦ : [C:\Program Files\PHP8\php-cgi.exe   ] [Browse...]

Arguments ⑦ : [   ]

Advanced Parameters ⑦ : [**Edit...**]

☑ Check for file existence before execution ⑦

Type ⑦ : [Standard   ⌄]

☑ Use the associated extensions to automatically update the Script Paths ⑦

Figure 7-16. *Setting Up*

Click "Add" in the "Associated Extensions" table, then enter php in the extension field. Click "OK," then click "OK" again (Figure 7-17).

Associated Extensions ⑦ :

Extension		
php	✎	🗑
	Add	

[OK]

Figure 7-17. *Associated Extensions Table*

Now we need to add the php extension to the index files.
Back on the main screen, click "Index Files" (Figure 7-18).

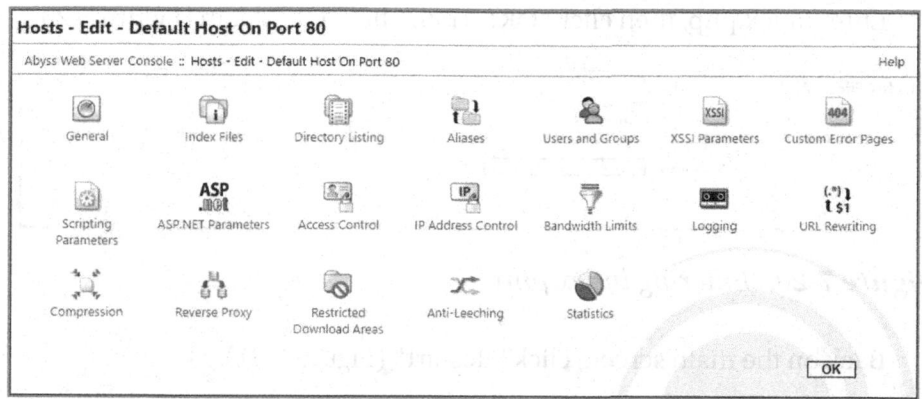

Figure 7-18. *Select Index Files*

Click "Add" on the bottom right of the "Index Files" section
(Figure 7-19).

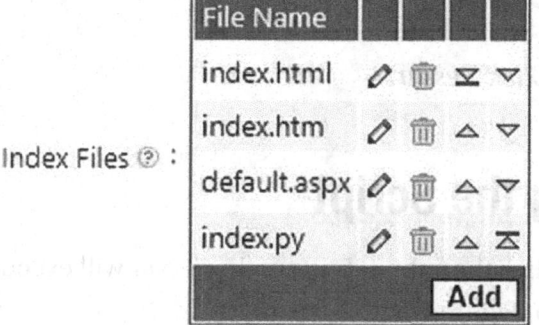

Figure 7-19. *Index Files Section*

Enter index.php, then click "OK." Then click "OK" again (Figure 7-20).

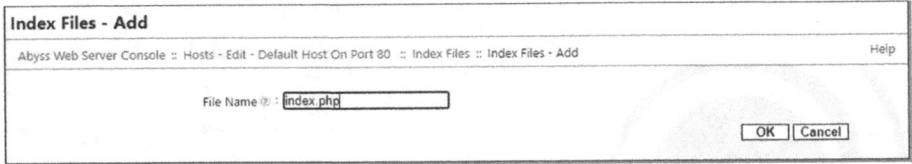

Figure 7-20. *Entering index.php*

Back on the main screen, click "Restart" (Figure 7-21).

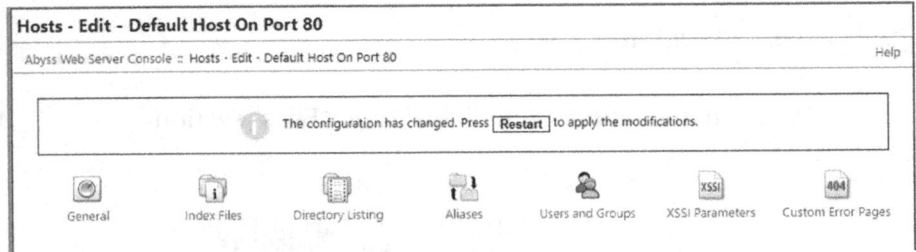

Figure 7-21. *Click Restart*

Executing the Script

Now when we click the submit button, the server will execute a PHP script called book.php (Figure 7-22).

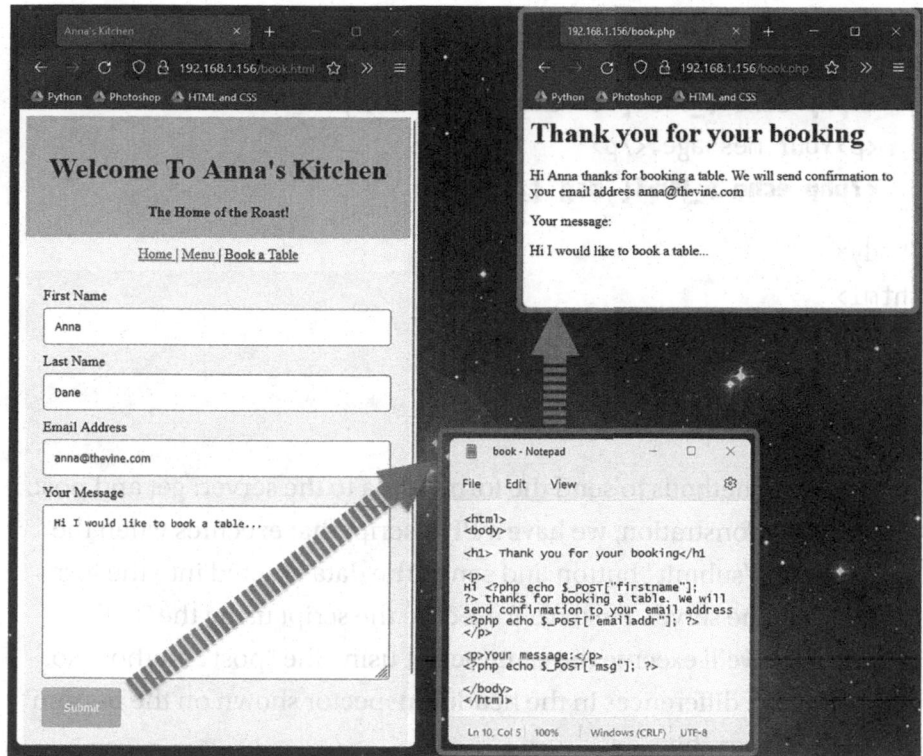

Figure 7-22. *The Script Executed After Submit Is Clicked*

I've included a sample PHP script called book.php that you can use to try out the form as follows:

```
<html>
<head>
    <title> Thanks for your booking</title>
</head>
<body>

<h1> Thank you for your booking</h1>
    <p>Hi <?php echo $_POST["firstname"]; ?>
```

thanks for booking a table. We will send confirmation to
your email address
`<?php echo $_POST["emailaddr"]; ?>``</p>`
`<p>Your message:</p>`
`<?php echo $_POST["msg"]; ?>`

```
</body>
</html>
```

Submission Method

There are two methods to send the form's data to the server: get and post.

In this demonstration, we have a PHP script that executes when the user clicks the "submit" button and sends the data entered into the form fields back to the server. First, we'll execute the script using the "get" method, then we'll execute the same script using the "post" method, so you can see the differences in the header inspector shown on the bottom right of the screenshots.

Get

The "get" method appends the inputted data to the requesting URL separated by a "?" (Figure 7-23). This is called a query string.

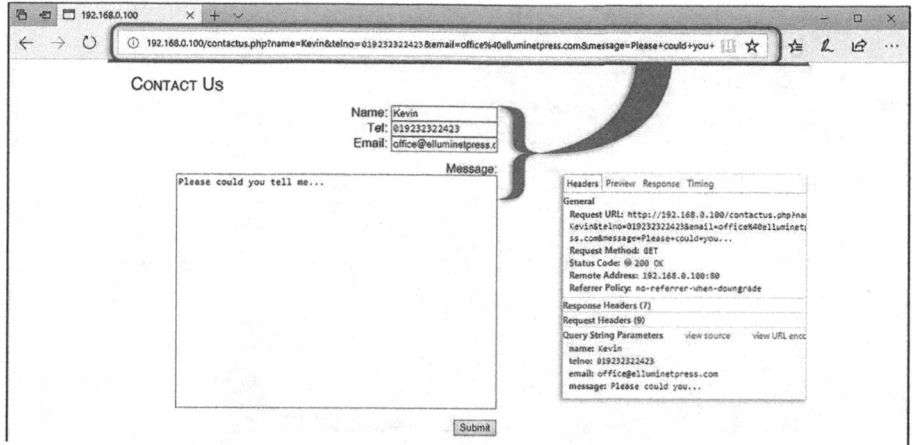

Figure 7-23. *Query String*

You can see the data appended to the URL of the script in the preceding illustration and the query string attributes in the header inspector.

This method should never be used to submit sensitive information like passwords as it is clearly visible on the page URL.

Post

Using the "post" method, all the data is sent with the HTTP headers of the processing script rather than through the URL. Notice that the URL in the address bar at the top of the browser is clean (Figure 7-24).

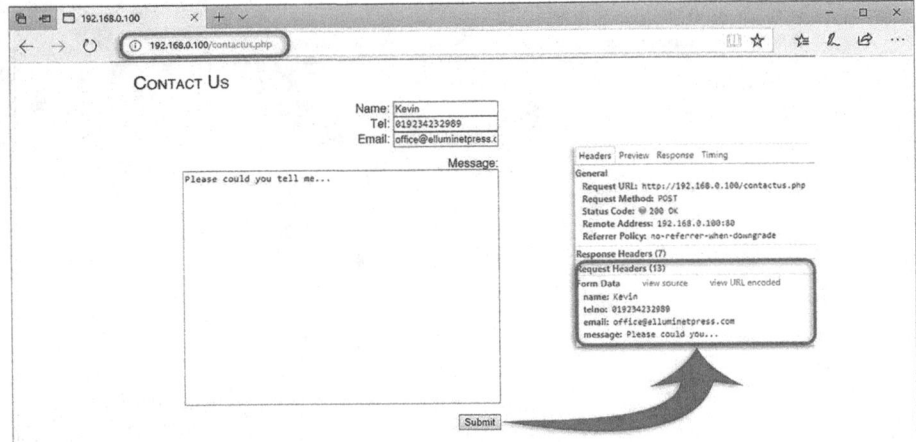

Figure 7-24. *Use of the Post Method*

You can see the data appended to the header of the script in the preceding illustration.

Lab Exercises

1. Create an HTML form to accept some information from a user such as name, email, etc.

2. Add some styling to make the form look a bit better.

3. What are the submission methods used to pass the data entered into the form to the server? Which should you use?

4. What is a query string?

5. How is the form data processed?

Summary

- Use <form action=" ">...</form> to create a form and specify the script to process the data.

- The "get" submission method appends the inputted data to the requesting URL.

- The "post" method sends the data with the HTTP headers of the processing script rather than through the URL.

CHAPTER 8

Introduction to JavaScript

Originally named LiveScript, JavaScript was developed by Brendan Eich at Netscape in the mid-1990s. It was later renamed JavaScript in 1995.

JavaScript is an interpreted, object-based, client-side scripting language that allows you to create dynamic content on a web page. You can animate images, validate data, and create interactive elements. In other words, JavaScript adds behavior to web pages, and it is supported by most modern web browsers such as Chrome, Firefox, Edge, and Safari.

There are three ways you can add JavaScript to a web page:

1. You can embed the code between <script> tags within your HTML document. You can add this to the <head> or <body> section of your HTML document. In the example in Figure 8-1, we've added the JavaScript code between the <script> tags in the header.

© Kevin Wilson 2023
K. Wilson, *The Absolute Beginner's Guide to HTML and CSS*,
https://doi.org/10.1007/978-1-4842-9250-1_8

```html
<!DOCTYPE html>
<html>

<head>
    <title>Welcome to JavaScript</title>

    <script>
        function mult(a, b) {
        document.getElementById("desc").innerHTML = a * b;
        }
    </script>

</head>

<body>
    <h1>Welcome to JavaScript</h1>

    <p id="desc"></p>

    <button type="button" onclick="mult(2, 2)">Multiply</button>
</body>

</html>
```

Figure 8-1. *Adding JavaScript*

2. You can save the JavaScript code in a separate file
   and link it to your HTML. This is useful for larger
   projects where you have multiple HTML documents
   using the same JavaScript functions.

   In this example, the JavaScript code is saved in the
   file script.js. We include the JavaScript file using the
   src attribute in the opening <script> tag. We can add
   this line in the header of the HTML file (Figure 8-2).

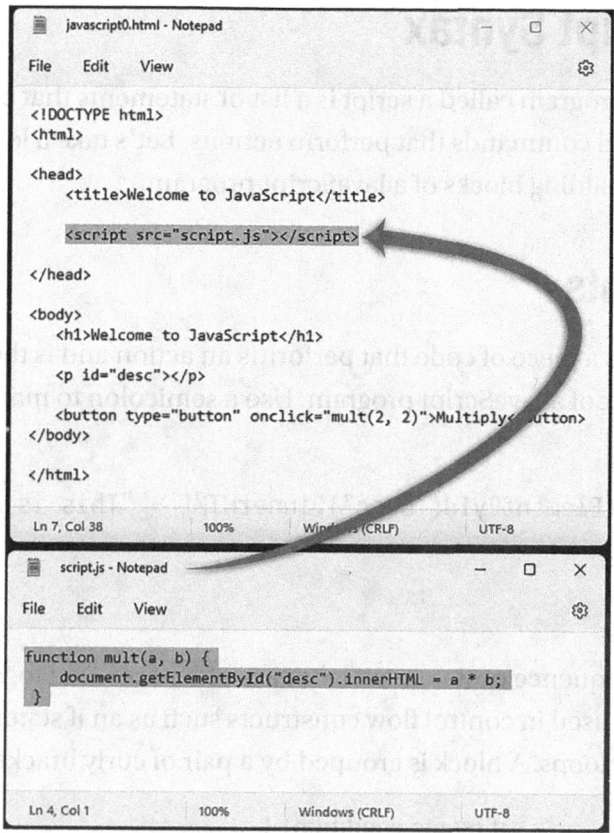

Figure 8-2. Adding JavaScript

3. You can also place the JavaScript code directly inside an HTML tag. This is known as inline code.

```
<a href="#" onClick="alert('Welcome !');"> Click
Here</a>
```

171

JavaScript Syntax

A JavaScript program called a script is a list of statements that contain constructs and commands that perform actions. Let's take a look at some of the basic building blocks of a JavaScript program.

Statements

A statement is a piece of code that performs an action and is the basic building block of a JavaScript program. Use a semicolon to mark the end of a statement:

```
document.getElementById("desc").innerHTML = "This is a test";
```

Blocks

A block is a sequence of statements that are often executed together and is commonly used in control flow constructs such as an if statement or in while and for loops. A block is grouped by a pair of curly brackets { }:

```
if (some condition) {
    statement 1;
    statement 2;      } Code block
    statement 3;
}
```

Identifiers

An identifier is a name you choose for variables, parameters, and functions. Here, we have declared a variable called firstNum:

```
let firstNum = 5;
```

Identifiers also identify function names. Here, we have a new function called addNum:

```
function addNum(n1, n2) {
  return n1 + n2;
}
```

Keywords

When using JavaScript, there are reserved keywords that have specific uses (Figure 8-3). Because of this, you cannot use any of the keywords as identifiers or property names.

abstract	delete	function	null	throw
boolean	do	goto	package	throws
break	double	if	private	transient
byte	else	implements	protected	true
case	enum	import	public	try
catch	export	in	return	typeof
char	extends	instanceof	short	var
class	false	int	static	void
const	final	interface	super	volatile
continue	finally	long	switch	while
debugger	float	native	synchronized	with
default	for	new	this	

Figure 8-3. JavaScript Keywords

Comments

Comments are ignored when the program is executed; however, you should always comment your code so anyone else can understand its function. You can add comments by enclosing the comment between /* and */.

```
/* This is a multiline comment and
      is often used to describe a section
      of code. */
```

If you just want to comment one line, use a //.

```
// this is a single-line comment
```

First Program

Let's take a look at an example. Here is a simple HTML page. We have enclosed the JavaScript code inside the <script> tags:

```
<!DOCTYPE html>
<html>

<body>
    <h1>Welcome to JavaScript</h1>

    <p id="desc"></p>

    <script>
        document.getElementById("desc").innerHTML = "This is
        a test";
    </script>

</body>

</html>
```

Let's put the JavaScript code into an HTML document (Figure 8-4). At the top, we've added a heading. We've also added the JavaScript code between the <script> tags in the body of the HTML document.

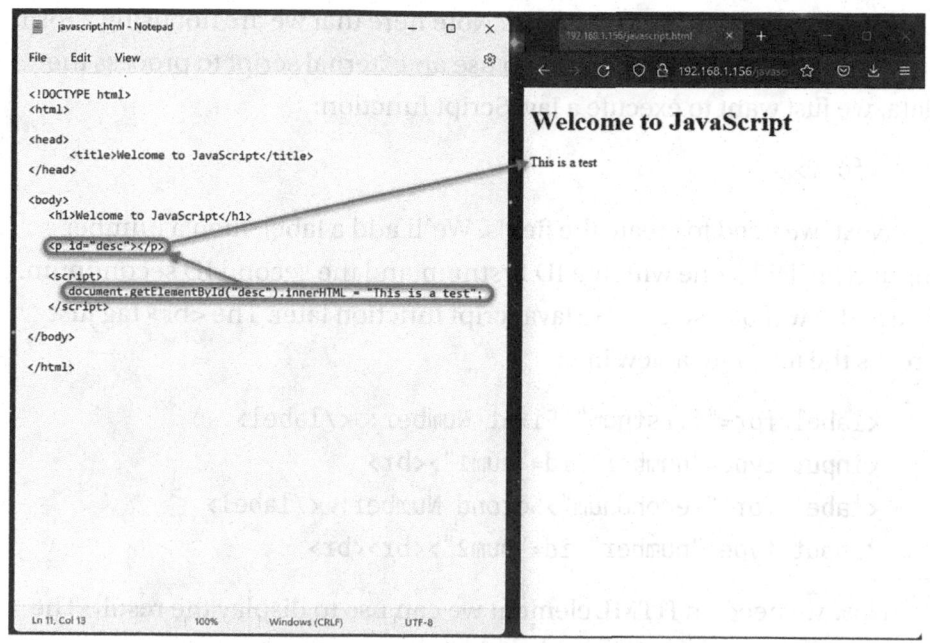

Figure 8-4. *Adding JavaScript Code to the HTML*

Here, we can see the getElementById() method assigns the text we specified to the object <p> in the document. This is how we can use JavaScript to manipulate an HTML document.

The getElementById method displays text output to the browser window. "So what," you say, "HTML already does that." Yes, it does, but using JavaScript you can do things you can't do with simple HTML. For example, you can display text or options based on variables or certain conditions. You can also use JavaScript to add interactivity and content validation to an otherwise static website.

Lab Exercise

In this exercise, we're going to create a small HTML form with a JavaScript function that adds two numbers and displays the result.

175

First, we need to build the form. Note here that we are not using a form submit handler as we don't need to use an external script to process the data, we just want to execute a JavaScript function:

```
<form>
```

Next, we need to create the fields. We'll add a label, then a number input type field – one with the ID firstnum and the second ID secondnum. These IDs will be used by the JavaScript function later. The <br> tag just breaks the text onto a new line:

```
<label for="firstnum">First Number: </label>
<input type="number" id="num1"><br>
<label for="secondnum">Second Number: </label>
<input type="number" id="num2"><br><br>
```

Now we need an HTML element we can use to display the result. The span element is a generic container for inline content:

```
<span id="res"></span> <br>
```

Next, we add a button for the user to click to add the values:

```
<input type="button" value="Add"
```

Now when the user clicks the button, this raises an onclick event. We need to tell the onclick event to run our function when the user clicks the button. So in the line we added earlier, we can add an onclick event and call the function:

```
<input type="button" value="Add" onclick="add();">
```

We'll end up with something like Figure 8-5.

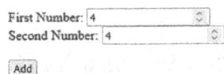

Welcome to JavaScript

Figure 8-5. HTML Form with JavaScript Function

176

After we've created the HTML page, we need to add the JavaScript. In this case, I'm going to add the JavaScript to the actual HTML page. We do this using the <script> tags.

Inside the script tags, first, we declare our function to add the numbers:

```
<script>
    function add () {
```

Next, we need to create a couple of variables to store the numbers so we can work on them. To do this, we need to retrieve the number that was entered into the fields on the form (num1 and num2). We can use the getElementById method to retrieve the value from num1 and num2 (Figure 8-6).

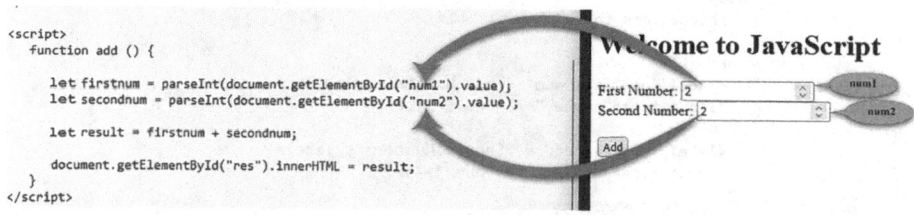

Figure 8-6. *Retrieving the Numbers*

Because the values entered into the form are text (a string), we need to convert these to a whole number (or integers). To do this, we use the parseInt() function. After conversion, these values are assigned to the variables firstnum and secondnum:

```
let firstnum = parseInt(document.getElementById("num1").
value);
let secondnum = parseInt(document.getElementById("num2").
value);
```

Next, we need to add the two numbers together and assign the answer to the variable result:

```
let result = firstnum + secondnum;
```

We can write the value of result to the HTML span element that has the ID "res":

```
document.getElementById("res").innerHTML = result;
```

Here, we see the value of result is assigned to the HTML value of the span element on the web page (Figure 8-7).

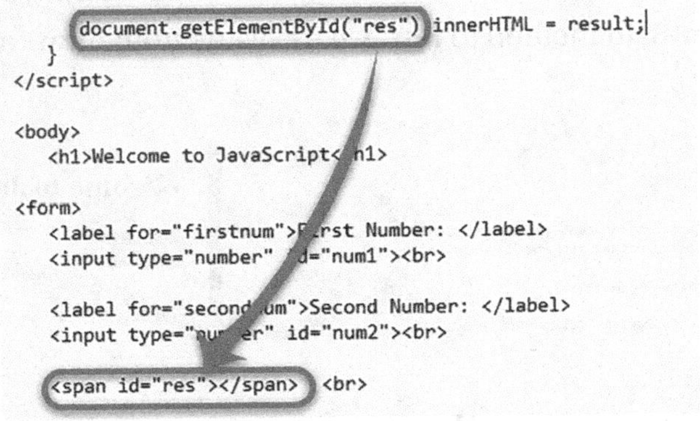

Figure 8-7. *Value Assigned to HTML*

Let's see how the code works when we open it in a browser. When you enter two numbers into the fields, once you click the button the add() function is called. The first two lines of the function get the values from the form fields (e.g., 2). Next, the values are converted to integers (using parseInt()) and assigned to firstnum and secondnum, respectively. The values are then added together, and the answer is assigned to result (Figure 8-8).

178

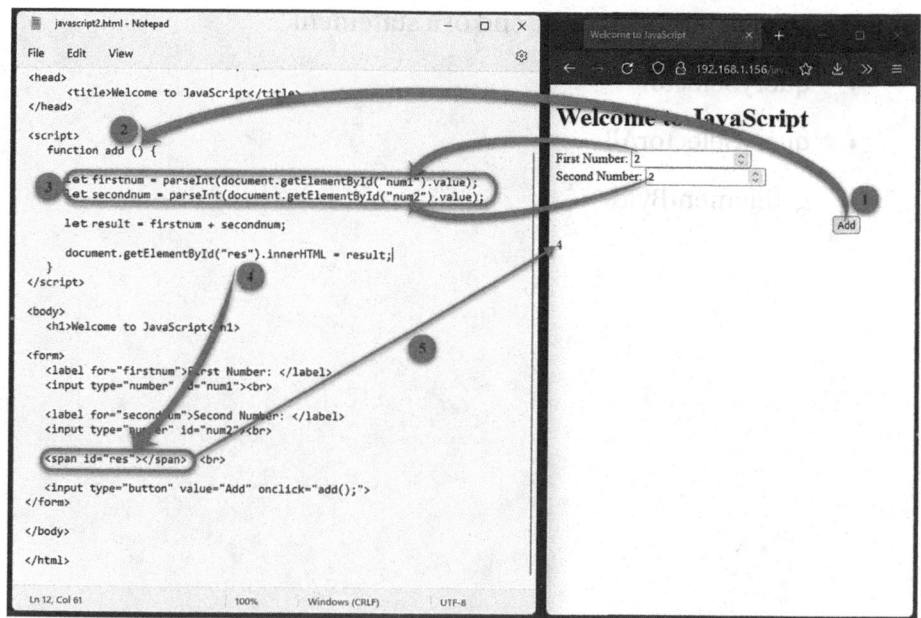

Figure 8-8. *Values Assigned to HTML*

The value in result is then assigned to the HTML value of the span element on the HTML page. This is what displays the result (in this example, "4").

Try it out.

Summary

- Embed the JavaScript code between <script>...</script> tags.

- Include an external script file using the src attribute in the opening <script> tag.

  <script src= "..."></script>

- A semicolon marks the end of a statement.

- querySelector

- querySelectorAll

- getElementById

CHAPTER 9

Content Management Systems

A content management system (or CMS) is a software application that enables you to create, edit, and store digital content. In other words, a CMS is a piece of software that runs on a web server and allows you to easily create, edit, and manage content published on a website.

The website data is stored in a database. The CMS platform takes care of all the technical aspects around building and managing a website. The end user can use a WYSIWYG text editor that looks like a word processor to create, publish, and edit content, without the need for coding experience. However, basic HTML and CSS knowledge is an advantage.

Most CMS platforms come with a selection of predesigned templates called themes that you can use to quickly customize the appearance of your site. You can also download countless other themes or even develop your own.

Nowadays, this is the most common way to build a website rather than using static HTML pages.

WordPress is by far the most popular content management system and powers roughly 43% of the websites on the Internet; however, there are others such as Drupal, Joomla, and Umbraco. You can find more detailed information on using these platforms on the following websites:

- wordpress.org

- drupal.org

© Kevin Wilson 2023
K. Wilson, *The Absolute Beginner's Guide to HTML and CSS*,
https://doi.org/10.1007/978-1-4842-9250-1_9

- joomla.org

- umbraco.com

Rather than creating static HTML pages, the website content is stored in a database (usually MySQL). The pages that you see when you visit the website are generated dynamically and formatted according to the theme used.

Using a CMS such as WordPress, websites can be created very quickly with the least amount of technical or programming expertise. Developers can develop plugins and themes for the website, and editors and publishers can log in and edit the content using a front end that looks similar to a word processor without the need to deal with code.

In Figure 9-1, we can see an editor on the back end of a WordPress website. The user can log in and add pages and blog posts to the site without having to use any code.

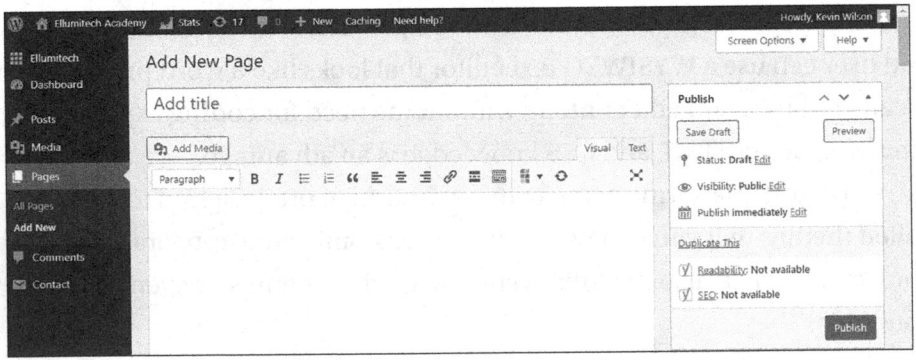

Figure 9-1. *WordPress Back End*

When someone visits the website, they'll see the published content (Figure 9-2). This is called the front end.

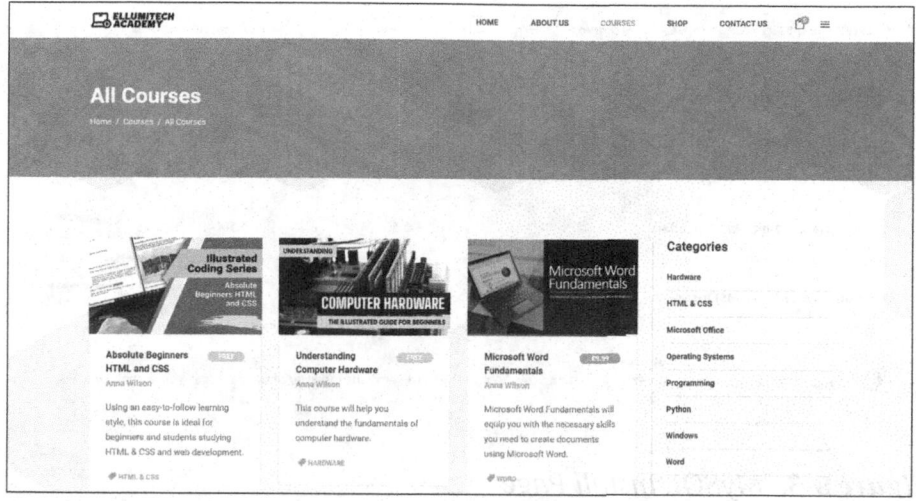

Figure 9-2. *WordPress Front End*

Set Up WordPress on Our Server

If you want to experiment with WordPress, you can download it from the following website:

`wordpress.org/download/`

Click "Download WordPress." This will download a zip file to your downloads directory.

You'll need to install PHP and configure it as we did in the "Configure the Web Server to Execute Scripts" section in Chapter 7.

Next, install MySQL. To do this, download the installer from the MySQL website:

`dev.mysql.com/downloads/installer/`

On the downloads page, next to "Windows (x86, 32-bit), MSI Installer, 5.5M," click "Download" (Figure 9-3).

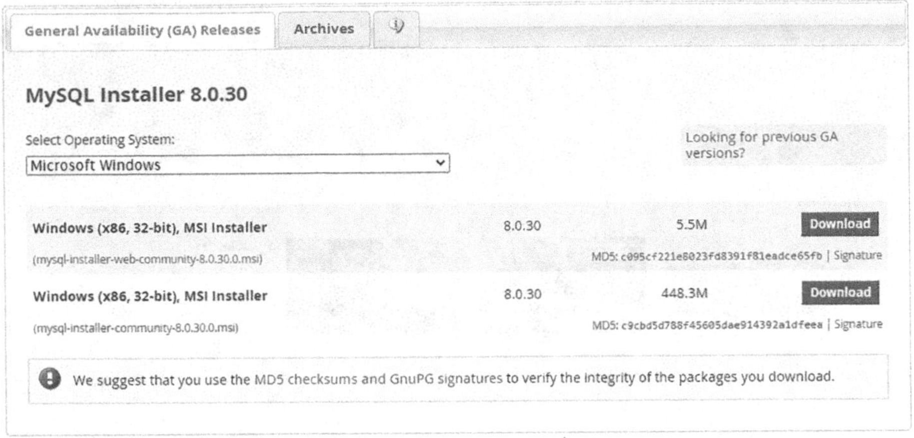

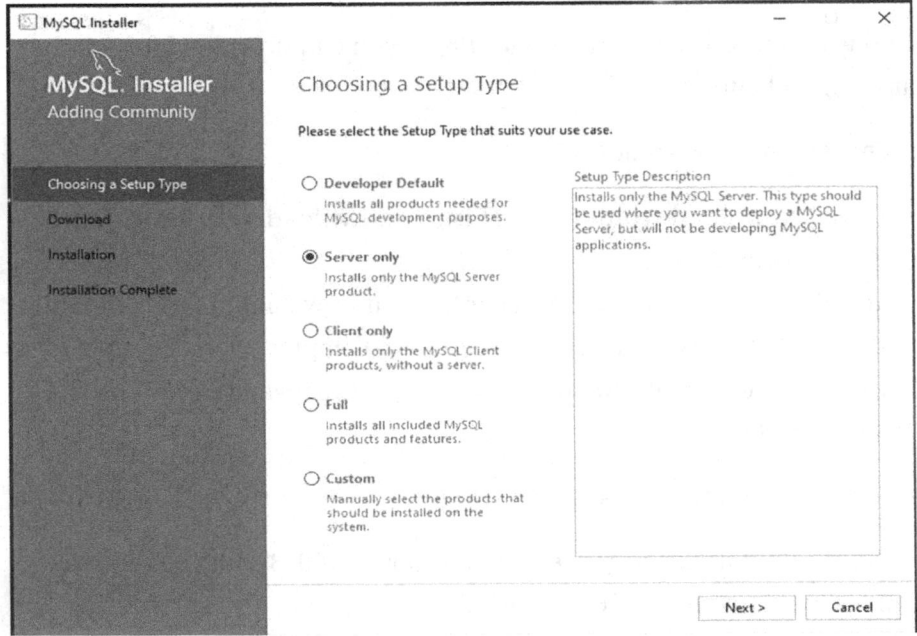

Figure 9-3. *MySQL Install Page*

Run the installer you just downloaded. You'll find it in your downloads folder. Run through the setup. When you get to the "Setup Type" screen, select "Server only," click "Next," then "Execute" (Figure 9-4).

Figure 9-4. *Setup Type Menu*

Select "Development Computer" from the "Type and Networking" options (Figure 9-5). Click "Next."

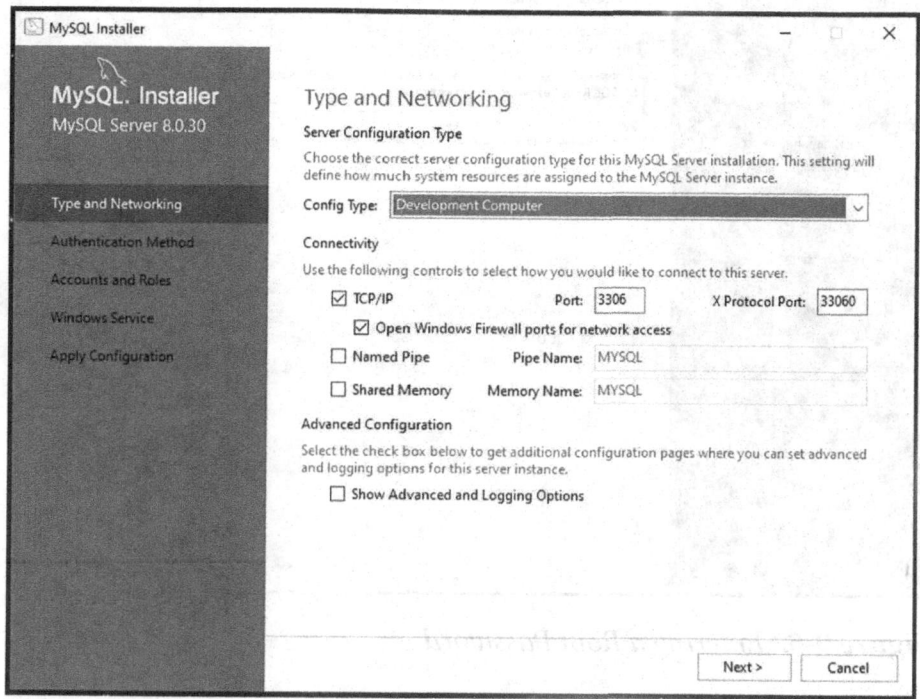

Figure 9-5. *Type and Networking Options Menu*

On the "Accounts and Roles" screen, enter a root password (Figure 9-6). This is the password you'll use to create and administer your databases, so don't forget it. Click "Next" to continue.

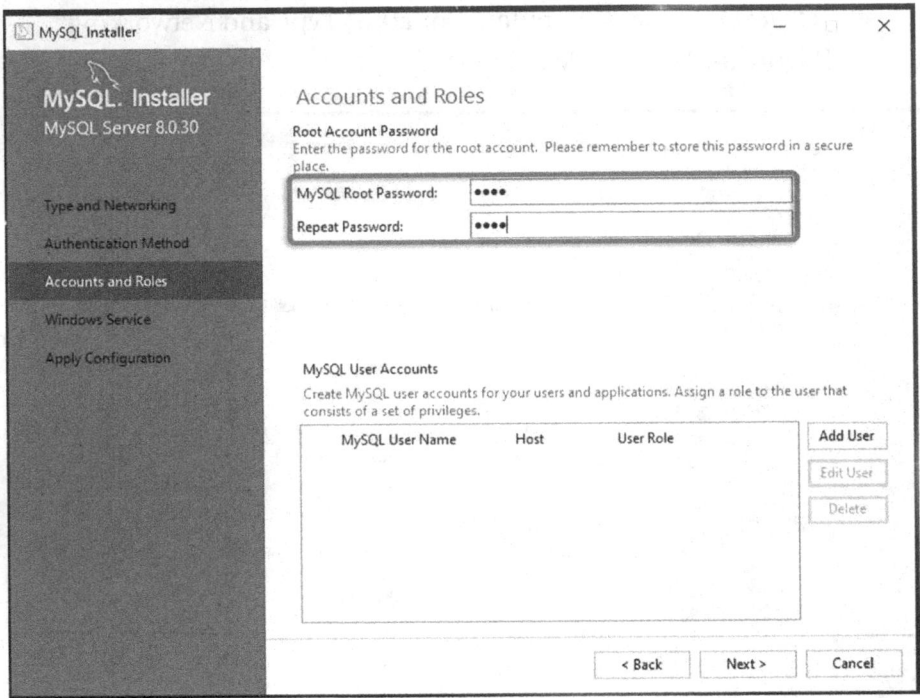

Figure 9-6. *Entering a Root Password*

Click "Next" on the "Windows Service" screen (Figure 9-7). You can leave these on the defaults.

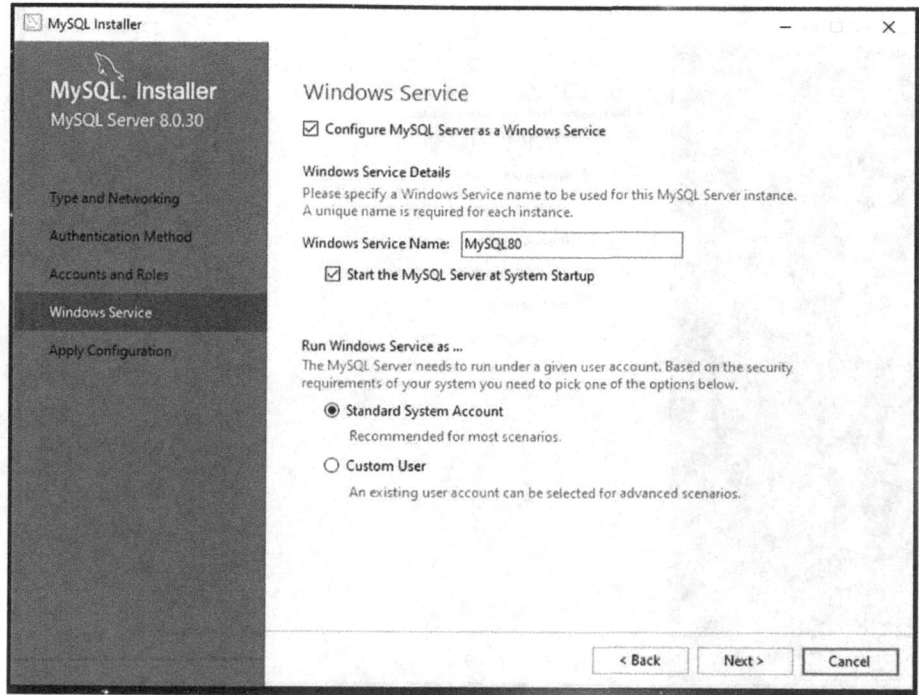

Figure 9-7. *Windows Service Menu*

Then click "Execute" to begin installation (Figure 9-8).

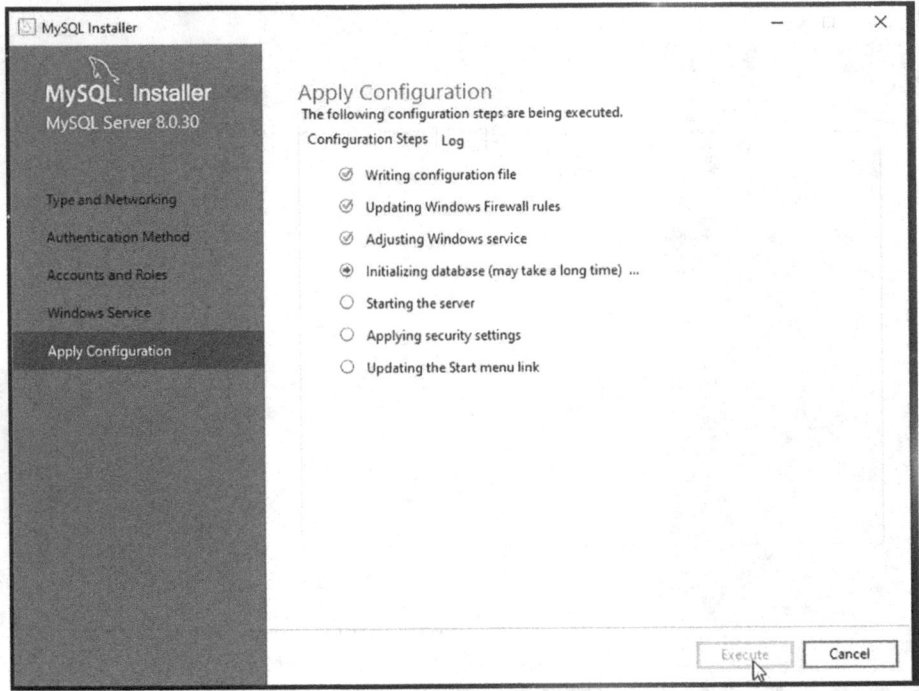

Figure 9-8. *Apply Configuration Menu*

Allow the software to install.

Now let's create our database. From the start menu, scroll down to "MySQL," then click "MySQL Command Line Client" (Figure 9-9).

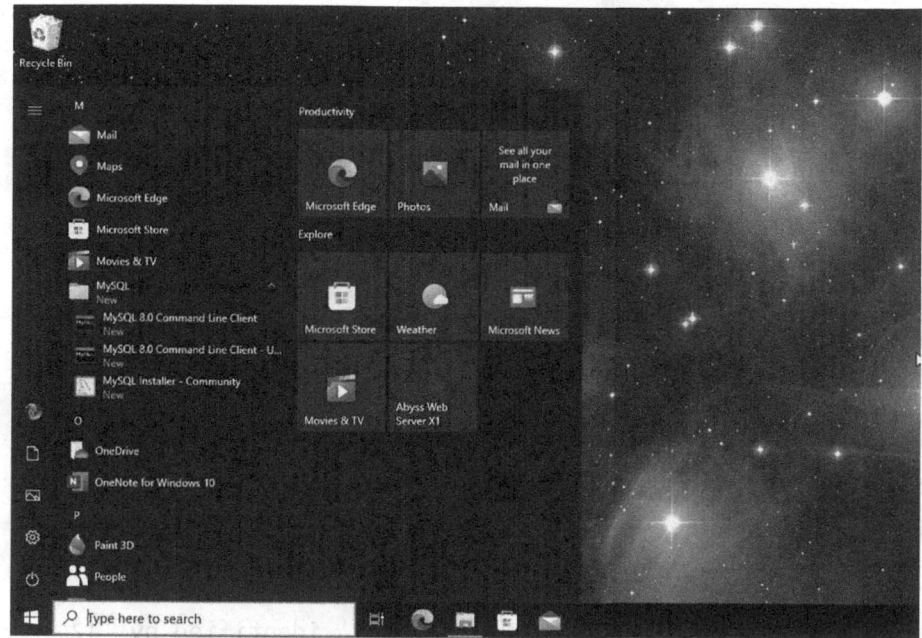

Figure 9-9. *MySQL Command Line Client in the Start Menu*

Enter the root password you chose when you installed the MySQL server (Figure 9-10).

Figure 9-10. *Enter the Root Password*

Now we need to create the database username that the WordPress site will use to connect to the database (Figure 9-11).

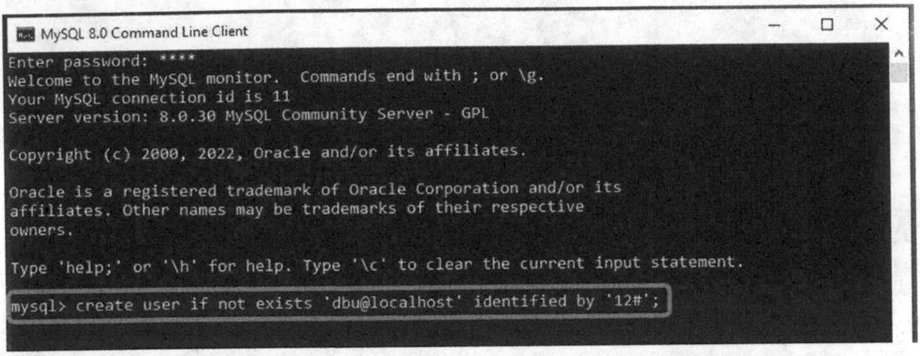

Figure 9-11. *Command Line Client*

Type the following at the MySQL command prompt:

```
create user if not exists 'dbu@localhost' identified by '12#'
```

This will create a user called dbu with a password of 12#. This is a simple example to demonstrate, but you should use a strong password instead.

Now we need to create the database. Type the following at the MySQL command prompt:

```
Create database if not exists 'mydb';
```

This will create a new database called mydb (Figure 9-12). Again, you should create a meaningful name for your database.

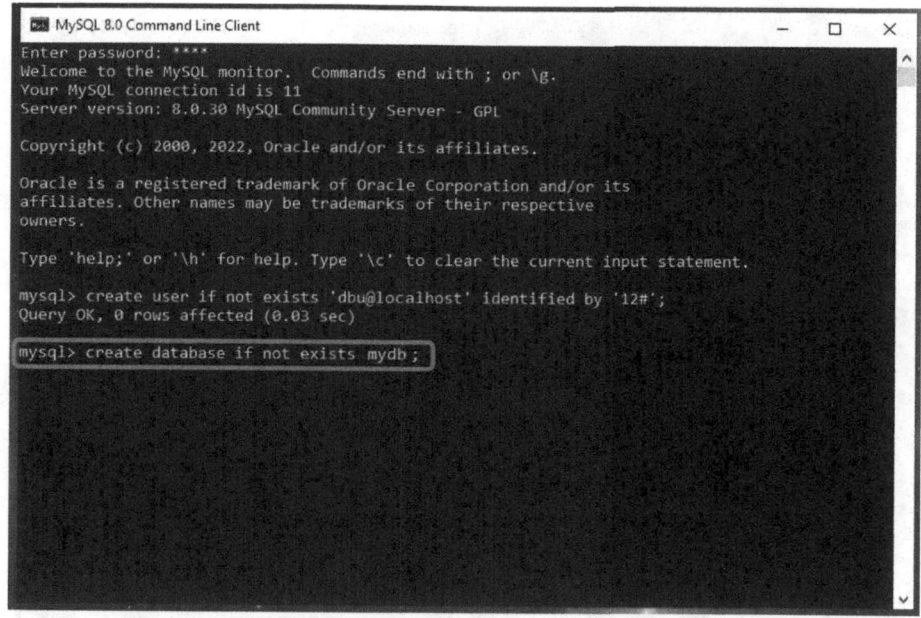

Figure 9-12. *Creating a Database*

Finally, we need to give permission to the user dbu we created earlier. Type the following line:

grant all privileges on mydb.* to 'dbu@hostname ';

Here, we're adding all privileges that WordPress needs to our user dbu to be able to access and use the mydb.

Next, we need to install WordPress.

Open file explorer, navigate to your downloads folder, right-click the WordPress zip file you downloaded earlier, and select "Extract All" from the pop-up menu (Figure 9-13).

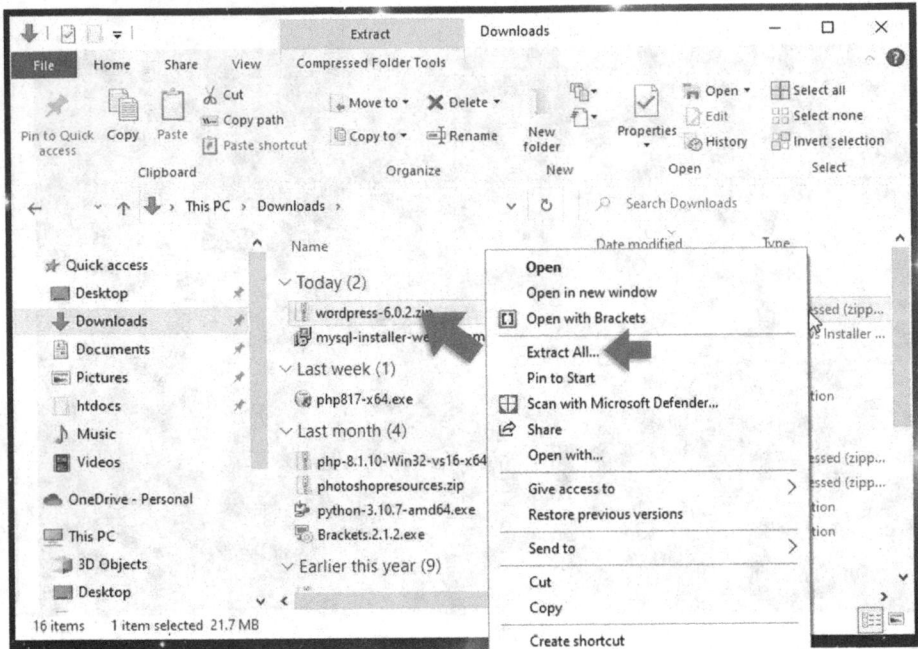

Figure 9-13. *Extract the WordPress Zip*

Enter the directory where the htdocs files for your web server are saved. When using Abyss, it will be C:\Abyss Web Server\htdocs (Figure 9-14).

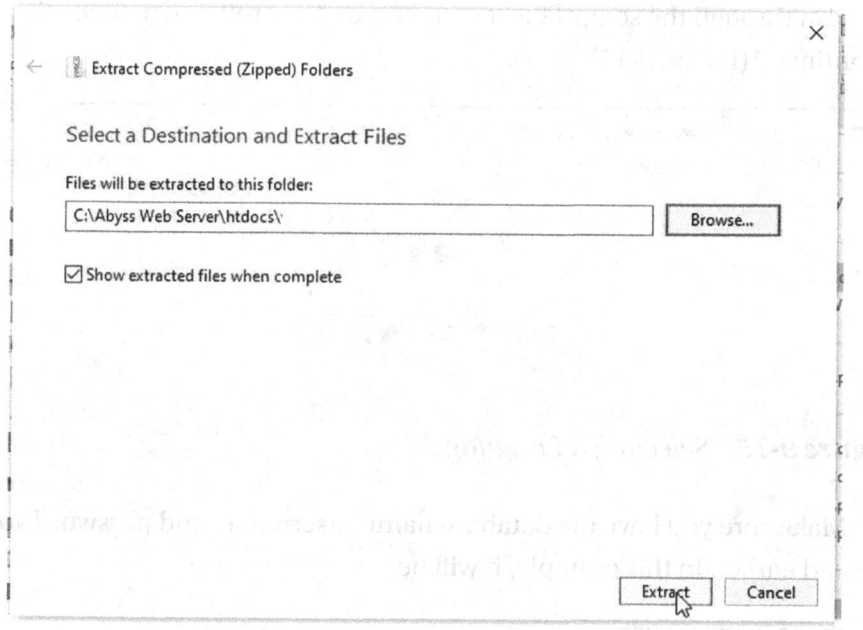

Figure 9-14. *Select a Destination in the Web Server*

Once the files have been extracted, open your web browser and navigate to

`127.0.0.1/wordpress`

Or if it doesn't work, try

`127.0.0.1/wordpress/wp-admin/setup-config.php`

Run through the setup. Select your language, scroll down, then click "Continue" (Figure 9-15).

Figure 9-15. *Selecting a Language*

Make sure you have the database name, username, and password you created earlier. In this example, it will be

```
Database name: mydb
User: dbu
Password 12#
```

Note, don't use simple passwords like this in a live website, use something stronger. I've just simplified the password so it's easier to understand.

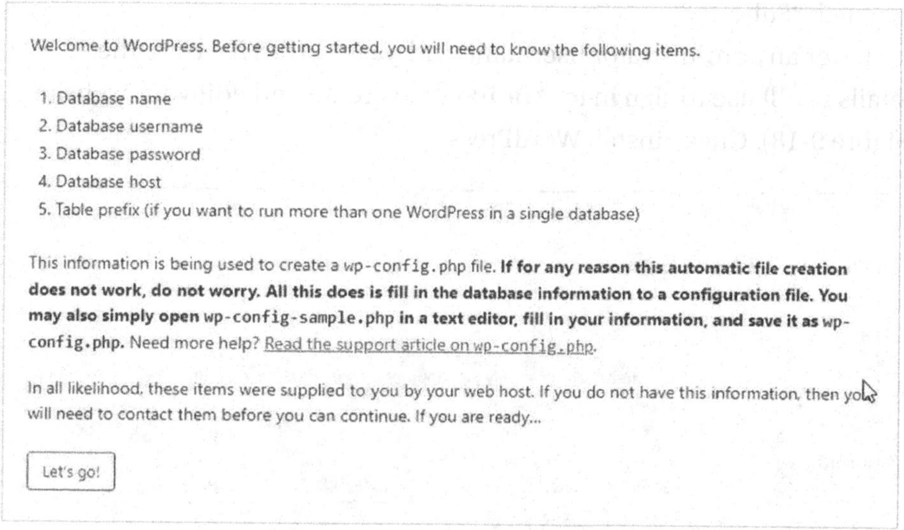

Welcome to WordPress. Before getting started, you will need to know the following items.

1. Database name
2. Database username
3. Database password
4. Database host
5. Table prefix (if you want to run more than one WordPress in a single database)

This information is being used to create a wp-config.php file. **If for any reason this automatic file creation does not work, do not worry. All this does is fill in the database information to a configuration file. You may also simply open wp-config-sample.php in a text editor, fill in your information, and save it as wp-config.php.** Need more help? Read the support article on wp-config.php.

In all likelihood, these items were supplied to you by your web host. If you do not have this information, then you will need to contact them before you can continue. If you are ready...

Let's go!

Figure 9-16. *WordPress Setup*

Click "Let's go!" (Figure 9-16).
Enter the details into the fields (Figure 9-17).

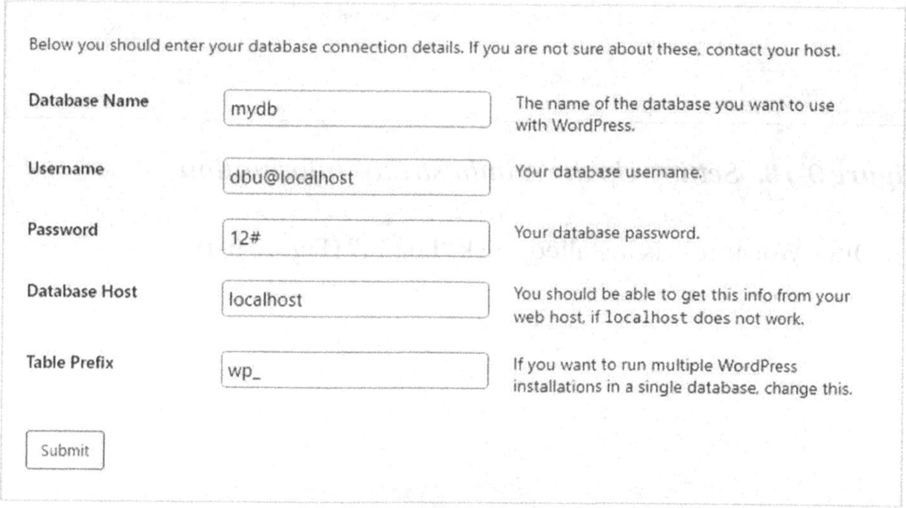

Below you should enter your database connection details. If you are not sure about these, contact your host.

Database Name	mydb	The name of the database you want to use with WordPress.
Username	dbu@localhost	Your database username.
Password	12#	Your database password.
Database Host	localhost	You should be able to get this info from your web host, if localhost does not work.
Table Prefix	wp_	If you want to run multiple WordPress installations in a single database, change this.

Submit

Figure 9-17. *Filling Out the Fields*

Click "Submit."

Enter an administrator username and password. These are the details you'll use to sign in to WordPress to create and edit your website (Figure 9-18). Click "Install WordPress."

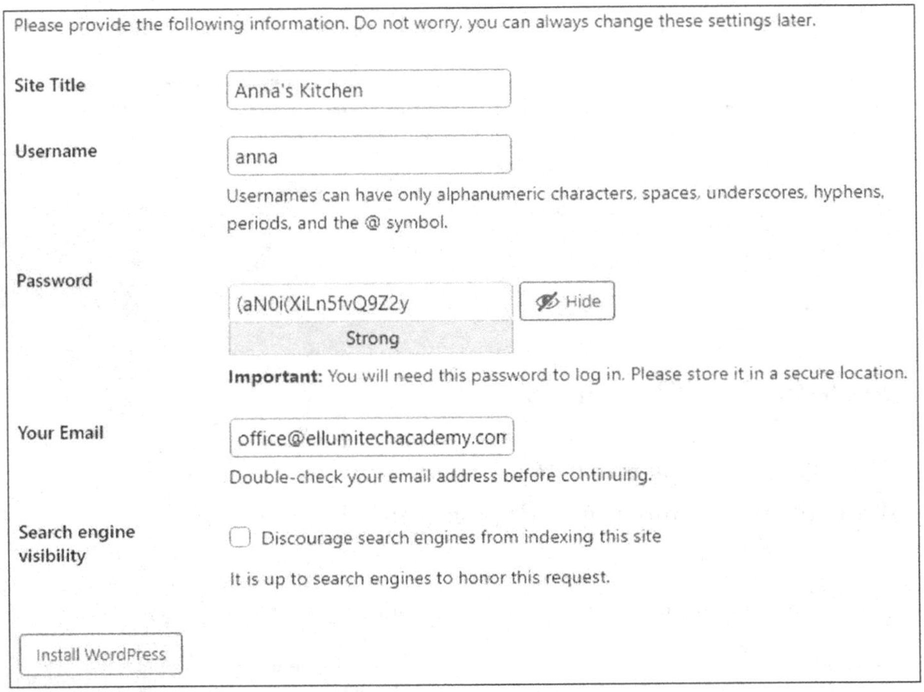

Please provide the following information. Do not worry, you can always change these settings later.

Site Title	Anna's Kitchen
Username	anna
	Usernames can have only alphanumeric characters, spaces, underscores, hyphens, periods, and the @ symbol.
Password	(aN0i(XiLn5fvQ9Z2y ◎ Hide
	Strong
	Important: You will need this password to log in. Please store it in a secure location.
Your Email	office@ellumitechacademy.com
	Double-check your email address before continuing.
Search engine visibility	☐ Discourage search engines from indexing this site
	It is up to search engines to honor this request.

Install WordPress

Figure 9-18. *Setting Up the Administrator Information*

Once WordPress is installed, click "Log In" (Figure 9-19).

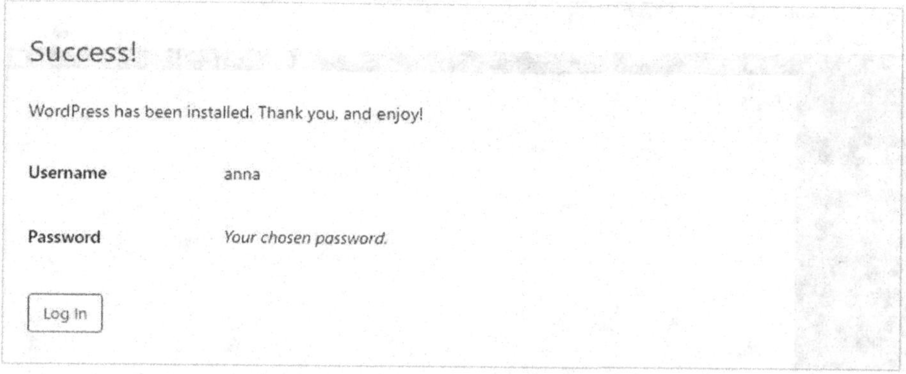

Success!

WordPress has been installed. Thank you, and enjoy!

Username   anna

Password   *Your chosen password.*

Log In

Figure 9-19. *Log In*

Enter the username and password you created when you installed WordPress (Figure 9-20).

Figure 9-20. *Enter Your Username and Password*

You'll land on the wp-admin dashboard (Figure 9-21).

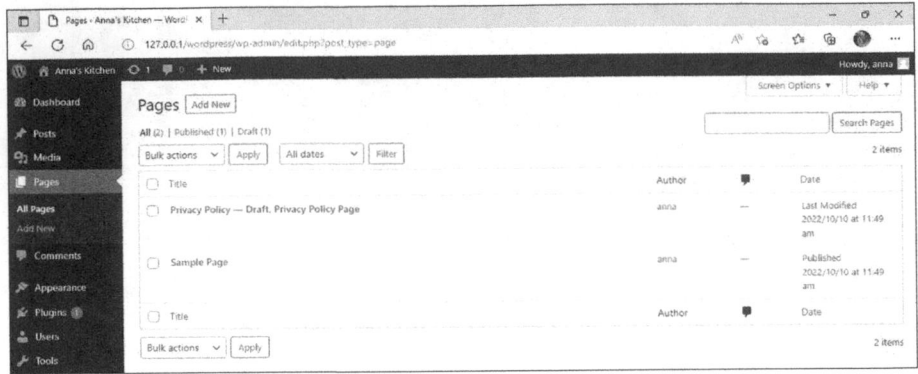

Figure 9-21. *Wp-Admin Dashboard*

You can access your site from

```
127.0.0.1/wordpress
```

For the administrator back end

```
127.0.0.1/wordpress/wp-admin
```

Have a look around WordPress and see how it works. Try some themes on the appearance tab on the left-hand side (Figure 9-22).

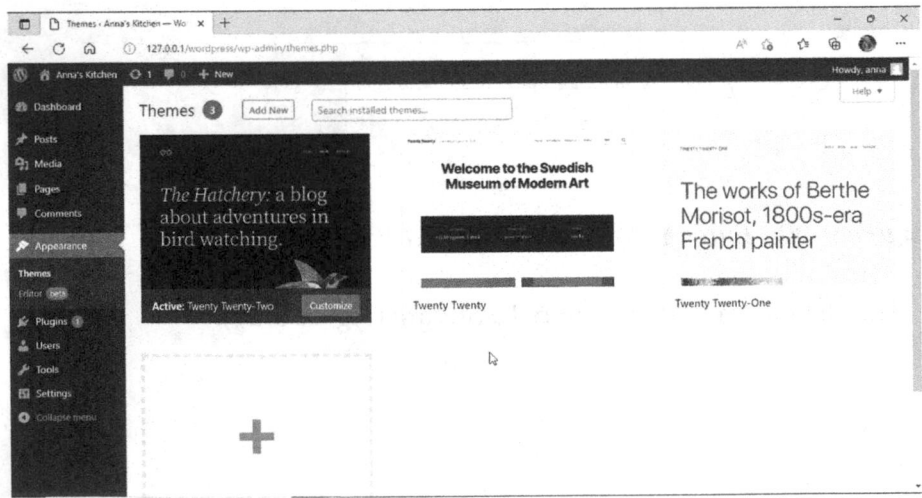

Figure 9-22. *Appearance Options*

Try adding some pages using the pages tab.

Web Development Frameworks

A web framework is a software platform for developing web applications and websites. These frameworks offer a wide range of prewritten components, code snippets, and application templates that can be used to develop web services and other web resources.

There are two types of frameworks – client side (front end) and server side (back end).

Front-end frameworks such as React and Angular are used to design the user interface of a website or application – the bit you can see when you visit the site. The front-end frameworks are mostly based on JavaScript, HTML, and CSS.

Back-end frameworks such as Flask and ASP.NET are used to design the hidden part of the app or website that is responsible for database management, security, URL routing, and page generation. These frameworks are based on Python, .NET, Ruby, Java, and PHP.

Another framework that is both a front end and a back end is Django, which is a prominent Python framework that is used by developers and businesses.

For more information on these frameworks, take a look at the websites listed in Table 9-1.

Table 9-1. *Framework Websites*

Framework	Website
Django	www.djangoproject.com
Flask	flask.palletsprojects.com
ASP.NET	dotnet.microsoft.com
Angular	angular.io
React	reactjs.org

Summary

- A content management system (or CMS) is a software application that enables you to create, edit, and store digital content.

- WordPress is by far the most popular content management system and powers roughly 43% of the websites on the Internet; however, there are others such as Drupal, Joomla, and Umbraco.

- Using a CMS such as WordPress, websites can be created very quickly with the least amount of technical or programming expertise. Developers can develop plugins and themes.

- You can download it from wordpress.org/download/.

- You can download MySQL from mysql.com/ downloads/windows/installer/.

- A web framework is a software platform for developing web applications and websites.

- Front-end frameworks such as React and Angular are used to design the user interface of a website or application.

- Back-end frameworks such as Flask and ASP.NET are used to design the hidden part of the app or website that is responsible for database management, security, URL routing, and page generation.

APPENDIX A

HTML Element Reference

A

<!-- -->	This tag is used to apply a comment in an HTML document	
<!DOCTYPE>	This tag is used to specify the version of HTML	<!DOCTYPE html>
<a>	It is termed as the anchor tag, and it creates a hyperlink or link	<a href = ""> link </a>
<abbr>	Defines an abbreviation for a phrase or longer word	<abbr title="full"> abbreviation </abbr>
<area>	Defines the area of an image map	<area shape="rect" coords=" " href=" ">
<article>	Defines the self-contained content	<article> ... </article>
<aside>	Defines content aside from the main content. Mainly represented as a sidebar	<aside> ... </aside>
<audio>	Used to embed sound content in an HTML document	<audio controls> <source src=" " type="audio/mpeg"> </audio>

© Kevin Wilson 2023
K. Wilson, *The Absolute Beginner's Guide to HTML and CSS*,
https://doi.org/10.1007/978-1-4842-9250-1

B

<b>	Used to make text bold	<b> ... </b>
<blockquote>	Used to define content taken from another source	<blockquote cite=" "> Quote... </blockquote>
<body>	Used to define the body section of an HTML document	<body> ...</body>
 	Used to apply a single line break	A line of text
<button>	Used to represent a clickable button	<button type = ""> button, reset, submit

C

<canvas>	Used to provide a graphics space within a web document	<canvas> ... </canvas>
<caption>	Used to define a caption for a table	<caption> ... </caption>
<center>	Used to align the content in the center	<center> ... </center>
<cite>	Used to define the title of a work, book, website, etc.	<cite> ... </cite>
<code>	Used to display a part of programming code in an HTML document	<code> ... </code>

D

`<datalist>`	Used to provide a predefined list for input options	`<datalist id=" ">`
		    `<option value=" ">`
		    …
		`</datalist>`

`<dd>`	Used to provide a definition/description of a term in a description list	`<dd> … </dd>`
`<del>`	Defines a text which has been deleted from the document	`<del> … </del>`
`<details>`	Defines additional details which a user can either view or hide	`<details> …` `</details>`
`<dfn>`	Used to indicate a term which is defined within a sentence/phrase	`<dfn> … </dfn>`
`<dialog>`	Defines a dialog box or other interactive components	`<dialog open> …` `</dialog>`
`<div>`	Defines a division or section within an HTML document	`<div class=" "> …` `</div>`
`<dl>`	Used to define a description list	`<dl> … </dl>`
`<dt>`	Used to define a term in a description list	`<dt> … </dt>`

E

`<em>`	Used to emphasize the content applied within this element	`<em> … </em>`
`<embed>`	Used as an embedded container for type text/html, image/jpg, video/mp4	`<embed type = " " src = " " width=" " height=" ">`

F

<fieldset>	Used to group related elements/labels within a web form	<fieldset> <legend> ... </legend> </fieldset>
<figcaption>	Used to add a caption or explanation for the <figure> element	<figcaption> ... </figcaption>
<figure>	Used to define the self-contained content and is mostly referenced as a single unit	<figure> ... </figure>
<footer>	Defines the footer section of a web page	<footer> ... </footer>
<form>	Used to define an HTML form	<form action = " " method = "post"> ... </form>

H

<h1> to <h6>	Defines headings for an HTML document from levels 1–6
<head>	Defines the head section of an HTML document
<header>	Defines the header of a section or web page
<hr>	Used to apply a thematic break between paragraph-level elements
<html>	Represents the root of an HTML document

I

\<i\>	Used to represent a text in some different voice	\<i\> … \</i\>
\<iframe\>	Defines an inline frame which can embed other content	\<iframe src=" " title=" " \> … \</iframe\>
\<img\>	Used to insert an image within an HTML document	\<img src= " " width = " " height = " "\>
\<input\>	Defines an input field within an HTML form. Types include text, tel, email, password, button, submit, checkbox, radio, etc.	\<input type="text" id=" " name=" "\>
\<ins\>	Represents text that has been inserted within an HTML document	\<ins\> … \</ins\>

K

\<kbd\>	Used to define keyboard input	\<kbd\> … \</kbd\>

L

\<label\>	Defines a text label for the input field of form	\<label for = " " \> … \</label\>
\<li\>	Used to represent items in a list	\<li\> … \</li\>
\<link\>	Links to an external resource such as a CSS file	\<link rel="stylesheet" type="text/css" href=" " /\>

M

\<main\>	Represents the main content of an HTML document	\<main\> ... \</main\>

\<map\>	Defines an image map with active areas	\<map name=" "\>
		    \<area shape="rect"
		    coords=" " href=" "\>
		\</map\>

\<mark\>	Represents a highlighted text	\<mark\> ... \</mark\>
\<meta\>	Defines metadata of an HTML document Name = description, keywords, author, viewport	\<meta charset="UTF-8"\> \<meta name=" " content=" "\>
\<meter\>	Defines scalar measurement with known range or fractional value	\<meter id=" " value=" " min=" " max=" "\> ... \</meter\>

N

\<nav\>	Represents a section of a page to represent navigation links	\<nav\> ... \</nav\>
\<noscript\>	Provides alternative content if a script type is not supported in a browser	\<noscript\> JavaScript not supported! \</noscript\>

O

\<object\>	Used to embed an object in an HTML file	\<object data=" " width=" " height=" "\> \</object\>
\<ol\>	Defines an ordered list of items	\<ol\> ... \</ol\>
\<optgroup\>	Used to group the options of a drop-down list	\<optgroup label=" "\> \<option value=" "\> ... \</option\> \<option value=" "\> ... \</option\> \</optgroup\>

P

\<p\>	Represents a paragraph in an HTML document	\<p style = ""\> ... \</p\>
\<pre\>	Defines preformatted text in an HTML document	\<pre\> ... \</pre\>
\<progress\>	Defines the progress of a task within an HTML document	\<progress id=" " value=" " max=" "\> ... \</progress\>

Q

\<q\>	Defines a short inline quotation	\<q\> ... \</q\>

S

\<s\>	Renders text which is no longer correct or relevant	\<s\> ... \</s\>
\<samp\>	Used to represent a sample output of a computer program	\<samp\> ... \</samp\>
\<script\>	Used to declare the JavaScript within an HTML document	\<script\> ... \</script\>
\<section\>	Defines a generic section for a document	\<section\> ... \</section\>

\<select\>	Represents a control which provides a menu of options	\<select name=" "
		id=" "\>
		  \<option value=" "\>
		  ...
		  \</option\>
		\</select\>

\<small\>	Used to make the text font one size smaller than a document's base font size	\<small\> ... \</small\>
\<source\>	Defines multiple media resources for different media elements such as \<picture\>, \<video\>, and \<audio\>	\<source src=" " type="audio/mpeg"\>
\<span\>	Used for styling and grouping inline elements	\<span\> ... \</span\>
\<strike\>	Used to render strikethrough text (not supported in HTML5)	\<strike\> ... \</strike\>
\<strong\>	Used to define important text	\<strong\> ... \</strong\>

(continued)

<style>	Used to contain CSS style information for an HTML document	<style> h1 {color:blue;} </style>
<sub>	Defines a text which displays as a subscript text	_{...}
<summary>	Defines a summary which can be used with the <details> tag	<summary> ... </summary>
<sup>	Defines a text which represents as a superscript text	^{...}
<svg>	Used as a container of SVG (Scalable Vector Graphics)	<svg width="" height=""> ... </svg>

T

<table>	Used to present data in tabular form or to create a table within an HTML document	<table> ... </table>
<tbody>	Represents the body content of an HTML table and used along with <thead> and <tfoot>	<tbody> ... </tbody>
<td>	Used to define cells of an HTML table which contains table data	<td> ... </td>
<template>	Used to contain the client-side content which will not display at the time of page load and may render later using JavaScript	<template> ... </template>

(continued)

<textarea>	Used to define multiple-line input, such as comment, feedback, review, etc.	<textarea id=" " name=" " rows=" " cols=" "> ... </textarea>
<tfoot>	Defines the footer content of an HTML table	<tfoot> ... </tfoot>
<th>	Defines the head cell of an HTML table	<th> ... </th>
<thead>	Defines the header of an HTML table. Used along with <tbody> and <tfoot> tags	<thead> ... </thead>
<time>	Used to define date/time within an HTML document	<time datetime="2022-02-24 21:00">
<title>	Defines the title or name of an HTML document	<title> ... </title>
<tr>	Defines the row cells in an HTML table	<tr> ... </tr>

U

<u>	Used to render enclosed text with an underline	<u> ... </u>
<ul>	Defines an unordered list of items	<ul> ... </ul>

V

<var>	Defines a variable name used in mathematical or programming context	<var> ... </var>
<video>	Used to embed a video content with an HTML document	<video width="" height="" controls> ... </video>

W

<wbr>	Defines a position within text where a break line is possible	<wbr> ... </wbr>

APPENDIX B

CSS Selector Reference

A

accent-color	Specifies an accent color for user interface controls	accent-color: Blue;
align-content	Specifies the alignment between the lines inside a flexible container when the items do not use all available space	align-content: center I start I end I normal I stretch I baseline;
align-items	Specifies the alignment for items inside a flexible container	align-items: center I start I end I normal I stretch I baseline;
align-self	Specifies the alignment for selected items inside a flexible container	align-self: center I start I end I normal I stretch I baseline;
all	Resets all properties (except unicode-bidi and direction)	all: initial I inherit I unset;

© Kevin Wilson 2023
K. Wilson, *The Absolute Beginner's Guide to HTML and CSS*,
https://doi.org/10.1007/978-1-4842-9250-1

B

background-color	Specifies the background color of an element	background-color: Grey
background-image	Specifies one or more background images for an element	background-image: url("...");
background-origin	Specifies the origin position of a background image	background-origin: padding-box | border-box | content-box | initial | inherit;
background-position	Specifies the position of a background image	background-position: left top | left center | left bottom | right top | right center | right bottom | center top | center center | center bottom
background-repeat	Sets if/how a background image will be repeated	background-repeat: repeat | repeat-x | repeat-y | no-repeat | initial | inherit;
background-size	Specifies the size of the background images	background-size: auto | length | cover | contain | initial | inherit;
border	A shorthand property for border-width, border-style, and border-color	border: border-width border-style border-color | initial | inherit;
border-color	Sets the color of the four borders	border-color: Red;
border-spacing	Sets the distance between the borders of adjacent cells. Use length to specify size	border-spacing: length | initial | inherit;

(continued)

border-style	Sets the style of the four borders	border-style: none I hidden I dotted I dashed I solid I double I inherit;
border-width	Sets the width of the four borders. Use length to specify size	border-width: length I initial I inherit I medium I thin I thick;
bottom	Sets the element's position from the bottom of its parent element. Use length to specify size	bottom: auto I length I initial I inherit;
box-shadow	Attaches one or more shadows to an element	box-shadow: none I h-offset v-offset blur spread color;

C

@charset	Specifies the character encoding used in the style sheet	@charset "UTF-8";
clear	Specifies what should happen with the element that is next to a floating element	clear: none I left I right I both I initial I inherit;
color	Sets the color of text	color: Green;
column-count	Specifies the number of columns an element should be divided into	column-count: 3;
column-fill	Specifies how to fill columns, balanced or not	column-fill: balance I auto I initial I inherit;
column-span	Specifies how many columns an element should span across	column-span: none I all I initial I inherit;

(continued)

column-width	Specifies the column width	
columns	A shorthand property for column-width and column-count	column-width: 100px;
cursor	Specifies the mouse cursor to be displayed when pointing over an element	cursor: pointer I help I wait I grab I n-resize;

D

display	Specifies how a certain HTML element should be displayed	display: inline I block;

F

float	Specifies whether an element should float to the left, right, or not at all	float: none I left I right I initial I inherit;
font	A shorthand property for the font-style, font-variant, font-weight, font-size/line-height, and font-family properties	font: 24px Roboto, sans-serif;
font-family	Specifies the font family for text	font-family: Helvetica;
font-kerning	Controls the usage of the kerning information (how letters are spaced)	font-kerning: auto I normal I none;
font-size	Specifies the font size of text. Use length to specify font size, e.g., 12px	font-size: small I medium I large I length I initial I inherit;

(continued)

font-style	Specifies the font style for text	font-style: normal I italic I oblique I initial I inherit;
font-weight	Specifies the weight of a font	font-weight: 900;font-weight: bold;

H

height	Sets the height of an element	height: 20px;

I

image-rendering	Specifies the type of algorithm to use for image scaling	image-rendering: auto I smooth I high-quality I crisp-edges I pixelated I initial I inherit;
@import	Allows you to import a style sheet into another style sheet	@import url ("…");@import "…";

J

justify-content	Specifies the alignment between the items inside a flexible container when the items do not use all available space	justify-content: flex-start I flex-end I center;

K

@keyframes	Specifies the animation code	@keyframes move {
		from {top: 0px;}
		to {top: 120px;}
		}

L

left	Specifies the left position of a positioned element	left: auto I 100px;
letter-spacing	Increases or decreases the space between characters in a text	letter-spacing: 2px;
line-break	Specifies how/if to break lines	line-break: auto I loose I normal I strict I anywhere;
line-height	Sets the line height	line-height: length;

M

margin	Sets all the margin properties in one declaration	margin: 5px;
margin-bottom	Sets the bottom margin of an element	margin-bottom: 5px;
margin-left	Sets the left margin of an element	margin-left: 5px;
margin-right	Sets the right margin of an element	margin-right: 5px;
margin-top	Sets the top margin of an element	margin-top: 5px;

(continued)

max-height	Sets the maximum height of an element	max-height: 110px;
max-width	Sets the maximum width of an element	max-width: 400px;

@media	Sets the style rules for different media types/devices/sizes	@media only screen and (max-width: 600px) {
		  body {
		    ...
		  }
		}

min-height	Sets the minimum height of an element	min-height: 100;
min-width	Sets the minimum width of an element	min-width: 600px;

O

object-position	Specifies the alignment of the replaced element inside its box. Use pos to specify the position	object-position: pos | initial | inherit;object-position: 5px 6px;
opacity	Sets the opacity level for an element. 0.0 is fully transparent; 1.0 is fully opaque	opacity: 0.5;
order	Sets the order of the flexible item, relative to the rest	order: number | initial | inherit;
outline	A shorthand property for the outline-width, outline-style, and outline-color properties	outline: 10px dotted red;
outline-color	Sets the color of an outline	outline-color: red;

(continued)

221

outline-offset	Offsets an outline and draws it beyond the border edge	outline-offset: 5px;
outline-style	Sets the style of an outline	outline-style: none | hidden | dotted | dashed | solid | double | groove | ridge | inset | outset;
outline-width	Sets the width of an outline	outline-width: 5px;
overflow	Specifies what happens if content overflows an element's box	overflow: visible | hidden | clip | scroll | auto | initial | inherit;
overflow-wrap	Specifies whether the browser can break lines with long words if they overflow beyond the container	overflow-wrap: normal | anywhere | break-word | initial | inherit;

P

padding	A shorthand property for all the padding properties	padding: 10px;
padding-bottom	Sets the bottom padding of an element	padding-bottom: 10px;
padding-left	Sets the left padding of an element	padding-left: 10px;
padding-right	Sets the right padding of an element	padding-right: 10px;
padding-top	Sets the top padding of an element	padding-top: 10px;
position	Specifies the type of positioning method used for an element	position: static | absolute | fixed | relative | sticky | initial | inherit;

R

resize	Defines how an element is resizable by the user	resize: none I both I horizontal I vertical I initial I inherit;
right	Specifies the right position of a positioned element	right: 10px;
row-gap	Specifies the gap between the grid rows	row-gap: 5px;

S

scroll-behavior	Specifies whether to smoothly animate the scroll position in a scrollable box, instead of a straight jump	scroll-behavior: auto I smooth I initial I inherit;

T

tab-size	Specifies the width of a tab character	tab-size: 10;
table-layout	Defines the algorithm used to lay out table cells, rows, and columns	table-layout: auto I fixed I initial I inherit;
text-align	Specifies the horizontal alignment of text	text-align: left I right I center I justify I initial I inherit;
text-decoration	Specifies the decoration added to text	text-decoration: overline I line-through I underline;

(continued)

text-decoration-color	Specifies the color of the text-decoration	text-decoration-color: red;
text-indent	Specifies the indentation of the first line in a text-block	text-indent: 40px;
text-shadow	Adds shadow to text	text-shadow: 2px 2px lightgrey;
top	Specifies the top position of a positioned element	top: 5px;

U

user-select	Specifies whether the text of an element can be selected	user-select: auto I none I text I all;

V

vertical-align	Sets the vertical alignment of an element	vertical-align: baseline I length I sub I super I top I text-top I middle I bottom I text-bottom I initial I inherit;
visibility	Specifies whether or not an element is visible	visibility: visible I hidden I collapse I initial I inherit;

W

width	Sets the width of an elementwidth: 150px;	width: auto I value I initial I inherit;
word-spacing	Increases or decreases the space between words in a text	word-spacing: 3px;
writing-mode	Specifies whether lines of text are laid out horizontally or vertically	writing-mode: vertical-rl;

APPENDIX C

CSS Color Codes

You can specify colors using the following formats:

- A Color keyword such as "red," "green," "blue," "transparent," "orange," etc.

- A hex value such as "#000000", "#00A500", "#FFFFFF", etc.

- An RGB value such as "rgb(255, 255, 0)"

Color Name	Hex Value	RGB Value
aliceblue	#F0F8FF	rgb(240, 248, 255)
antiquewhite	#FAEBD7	rgb(250, 235, 215)
aqua	#00FFFF	rgb(0, 255, 255)
aquamarine	#7FFFD4	rgb(127, 255, 212)
azure	#F0FFFF	rgb(1240, 255, 255)
beige	#F5F5DC	rgb(245, 245, 220)
bisque	#FFE4C4	rgb(255, 228, 196)
black	#000000	rgb(0, 0, 0)
blanchedalmond	#FFEBCD	rgb(255, 235, 205)
blue	#0000FF	rgb(0, 0, 255)

(continued)

© Kevin Wilson 2023
K. Wilson, *The Absolute Beginner's Guide to HTML and CSS*,
https://doi.org/10.1007/978-1-4842-9250-1

Color Name	Hex Value	RGB Value
blueviolet	#8A2BE2	rgb(138, 43, 226)
brown	#A52A2A	rgb(165, 42, 42)
burlywood	#DEB887	rgb(222, 184, 135)
cadetblue	#5F9EA0	rgb(95, 158, 160)
chartreuse	#7FFF00	rgb(95, 158, 160)
chocolate	#D2691E	rgb(210, 105, 30)
coral	#FF7F50	rgb(255, 127, 80)
cornflowerblue	#6495ED	rgb(100, 149, 237)
cornsilk	#FFF8DC	rgb(255, 248, 220)
crimson	#DC143C	rgb(220, 20, 60)
cyan	#00FFFF	rgb(0, 255, 255)
darkblue	#00008B	rgb(0, 0, 139)
darkcyan	#008B8B	rgb(0, 139, 139)
darkgoldenrod	#B8860B	rgb(184, 134, 11)
darkgray	#A9A9A9	rgb(169, 169, 169)
darkgreen	#006400	rgb(0, 100, 0)
darkkhaki	#BDB76B	rgb(189, 183, 107)
darkmagenta	#8B008B	rgb(139, 0, 139)
darkolivegreen	#556B2F	rgb(85, 107, 47)
darkorange	#FF8C00	rgb(255, 140, 0)
darkorchid	#9932CC	rgb(153, 50, 204)
darkred	#8B0000	rgb(139, 0, 0)
darksalmon	#E9967A	rgb(233, 150, 122)

(continued)

Color Name	Hex Value	RGB Value
darkseagreen	#8FBC8F	rgb(143, 188, 143)
darkslateblue	#483D8B	rgb(72, 61, 139)
darkslategray	#2F4F4F	rgb(47, 79, 79)
darkturquoise	#00CED1	rgb(0, 206, 209)
darkviolet	#9400D3	rgb(148, 0, 211)
deeppink	#FF1493	rgb(255, 20, 147)
deepskyblue	#00BFFF	rgb(0, 191, 255)
dimgray	#696969	rgb(0, 191, 255)
dodgerblue	#1E90FF	rgb(30, 144, 255)
firebrick	#B22222	rgb(178, 34, 34)
floralwhite	#FFFAF0	rgb(255, 250, 240)
forestgreen	#228B22	rgb(34, 139, 34)
fuchsia	#FF00FF	rgb(255, 0, 255)
gainsboro	#DCDCDC	rgb(220, 220, 220)
ghostwhite	#F8F8FF	rgb(248, 248, 255)
gold	#FFD700	rgb(255, 215, 0)
goldenrod	#DAA520	rgb(218, 165, 32)
gray	#808080	rgb(128, 128, 128)
green	#008000	rgb(0, 128, 0)
greenyellow	#ADFF2F	rgb(173, 255, 47)
honeydew	#F0FFF0	rgb(240, 255, 240)
hotpink	#FF69B4	rgb(255, 105, 180)
indianred	#CD5C5C	rgb(205, 92, 92)

(continued)

Color Name	Hex Value	RGB Value
indigo	#4B0082	rgb(75, 0, 130)
ivory	#FFFFF0	rgb(255, 255, 240)
khaki	#F0E68C	rgb(240, 230, 140)
lavender	#E6E6FA	rgb(230, 230, 250)
lavenderblush	#FFF0F5	rgb(255, 240, 245)
lawngreen	#7CFC00	rgb(124, 252, 0)
lemonchiffon	#FFFACD	rgb(255, 250, 205)
lightblue	#ADD8E6	rgb(173, 216, 230)
lightcoral	#F08080	rgb(240, 128, 128)
lightcyan	#E0FFFF	rgb(224, 255, 255)
lightgoldenrodyellow	#FAFAD2	rgb(250, 250, 210)
lightgreen	#90EE90	rgb(144, 238, 144)
lightgrey	#D3D3D3	rgb(211, 211, 211)
lightpink	#FFB6C1	rgb(255, 182, 193)
lightsalmon	#FFA07A	rgb(255, 160, 122)
lightseagreen	#20B2AA	rgb(32, 178, 170)
lightskyblue	#87CEFA	rgb(135, 206, 250)
lightslategray	#778899	rgb(119, 136, 153)
lightsteelblue	#B0C4DE	rgb(176, 196, 222)
lightyellow	#FFFFE0	rgb(255, 255, 224)
lime	#00FF00	rgb(0, 255, 0)
limegreen	#32CD32	rgb(50, 205, 50)
linen	#FAF0E6	rgb(250, 240, 230)

(continued)

Color Name	Hex Value	RGB Value
magenta	#FF00FF	rgb(255, 0, 255)
maroon	#800000	rgb(128, 0, 0)
mediumaquamarine	#66CDAA	rgb(102, 205, 170)
mediumblue	#0000CD	rgb(0, 0, 205)
mediumorchid	#BA55D3	rgb(186, 85, 211)
mediumpurple	#9370DB	rgb(147, 112, 219)
mediumseagreen	#3CB371	rgb(60, 179, 113)
mediumslateblue	#7B68EE	rgb(123, 104, 238)
mediumspringgreen	#00FA9A	rgb(0, 250, 154)
mediumturquoise	#48D1CC	rgb(72, 209, 204)
mediumvioletred	#C71585	rgb(199, 21, 133)
midnightblue	#191970	rgb(25, 25, 112)
mintcream	#F5FFFA	rgb(245, 255, 250)
mistyrose	#FFE4E1	rgb(255, 228, 225)
moccasin	#FFE4B5	rgb(255, 228, 181)
navajowhite	#FFDEAD	rgb(255, 222, 173)
navy	#000080	rgb(0, 0, 128)
navyblue	#9FAFDF	rgb(159, 175, 223)
oldlace	#FDF5E6	rgb(253, 245, 230)
olive	#808000	rgb(128, 128, 0)
olivedrab	#6B8E23	rgb(107, 142, 35)
orange	#FFA500	rgb(255, 165, 0)
orangered	#FF4500	rgb(255, 69, 0)

(*continued*)

Color Name	Hex Value	RGB Value
orchid	#DA70D6	rgb(218, 112, 214)
palegoldenrod	#EEE8AA	rgb(238, 232, 170)
palegreen	#98FB98	rgb(152, 251, 152)
paleturquoise	#AFEEEE	rgb(175, 238, 238)
palevioletred	#DB7093	rgb(219, 112, 147)
papayawhip	#FFEFD5	rgb(255, 239, 213)
peachpuff	#FFDAB9	rgb(255, 218, 185)
peru	#CD853F	rgb(205, 133, 63)
pink	#FFC0CB	rgb(255, 192, 203)
plum	#DDA0DD	rgb(221, 160, 221)
powderblue	#B0E0E6	rgb(176, 224, 230)
purple	#800080	rgb(128, 0, 128)
red	#FF0000	rgb(255, 0, 0)
rosybrown	#BC8F8F	rgb(188, 143, 143)
royalblue	#4169E1	rgb(65, 105, 225)
saddlebrown	#8B4513	rgb(139, 69, 19)
salmon	#FA8072	rgb(250, 128, 114)
sandybrown	#FA8072	rgb(244, 164, 96)
seagreen	#2E8B57	rgb(46, 139, 87)
seashell	#FFF5EE	rgb(255, 245, 238)
sienna	#A0522D	rgb(160, 82, 45)
silver	#C0C0C0	rgb(192, 192, 192)
skyblue	#87CEEB	rgb(135, 206, 235)

(continued)

Color Name	Hex Value	RGB Value
slateblue	#6A5ACD	rgb(106, 90, 205)
slategray	#708090	rgb(112, 128, 144)
snow	#FFFAFA	rgb(255, 250, 250)
springgreen	#00FF7F	rgb(0, 255, 127)
steelblue	#4682B4	rgb(70, 130, 180)
tan	#D2B48C	rgb(210, 180, 140)
teal	#008080	rgb(0, 128, 128)
thistle	#D8BFD8	rgb(216, 191, 216)
tomato	#FF6347	rgb(255, 99, 71)
turquoise	#40E0D0	rgb(64, 224, 208)
violet	#EE82EE	rgb(238, 130, 238)
wheat	#F5DEB3	rgb(245, 222, 179)
white	#FFFFFF	rgb(255, 255, 255)
whitesmoke	#F5F5F5	rgb(245, 245, 245)
yellow	#FFFF00	rgb(255, 255, 0)
yellowgreen	#9ACD32	rgb(139, 205, 50)

Index

A

Abyss Web Server, 9, 10, 13–15,
43, 44, 156
Adobe Dreamweaver IDE, 20
Anchor element, 34–37

B

Border radius, 129, 130, 154, 155
Box Model, 88, 90
Brackets, 19, 21, 22, 34, 123, 172
Browser window, 32, 33, 36, 44, 95,
102, 175
Buttons, 130
  cursor changes, 130, 131
  cursor property, 130
  hover state, 130
  radio buttons, 150

C

Cascading style sheets (CSS), 1,
7, 8, 75
  absolute and relative, 87
  attribute selector, 123
  box model, 88
  browser window, 124

class selectors, 80, 96
color codes, 87, 227
colors, 85
columns, 117
container, 91
element, 80
font and color, 84
font color and alignment, 85
grid, 105, 107, 115, 126
grouping selectors, 82
H1 tags, 83
hex value, 86
.highlight class, 81
HTML code, 75, 78, 80, 94
ID selectors, 81, 125
inline styles, 77
keyword, 85
layouts and sections, 90
rgb() function, 86
selector reference, 215
selectors, 79
sidebar, 106
style attribute, 76
styles, 79
symbol, 95
syntax, 78
text file and link, 76

© Kevin Wilson 2023
K. Wilson, *The Absolute Beginner's Guide to HTML and CSS*,
https://doi.org/10.1007/978-1-4842-9250-1

Y, Z

Printed in the United States
by Baker & Taylor Publisher Services

Printed in the United States
by Baker & Taylor Publisher Services